Creative Ways with Polymer Clay

Creative Ways with Polymer Clay

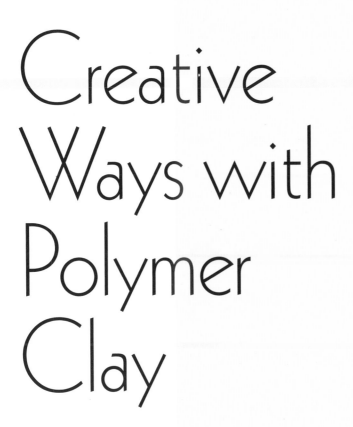

DOTTY McMILLAN

Sterling Publishing Co., Inc.
New York

This book is dedicated to all of the wonderful polymer clay pioneers who have been so gracious in sharing the knowledge they have worked so hard to acquire. Their efforts have been responsible for the incredible progress that has been made in such a short period of time in the art of polymer clay.

ACKNOWLEDGMENTS

So many people have helped me in the preparation of this book that I can't possibly mention them all. However, I am most grateful to all the members of the Orange County Polymer Clay Guild, the San Diego Polymer Clay Guild, and Marie and Howard Segal of the Clay Factory, for their friendship, their sharing, and their encouragement.

A special thank-you to Trina Williams, Judith Cook, and Debra Harvey Kunce for their helping hands; to Syndee Holt and all the members of the San Diego Polymer Clay Guild; to my husband, Al, for his constant help and encouragement; and to the entire polymer clay community for such a profusion of inspiration, excitement, and creativity. And last, but certainly not least, I'm most grateful for all the wonderful teachers I've had the privilege of learning from, including: Z Kripke, Sarajane Helm, Margaret Maggio, Kathy Dustin, Kathy Amt, Lindly Haunani, Nan Roche, Dan Cormier, Gwen Gibson, Marie Segal, Pier Voulkos, Mike Buesseler, Susan Hyde, Celie Fago, and Tory Hughes.

A very special thank-you goes to Nan Roche, whose book, *The New Clay,* has been the most impressive springboard into an art form that I have ever seen.

PHOTO CREDITS: Photos by Michael Hnatov and Kenneth Paul, Sr., for Michael Hnatov Photography, New York, except as follows:
Dotty McMillan: 8L; 22L; 24L; 25; 32R; 33; 34; 35R (lower); 37 top; 39R; 40; 41R (lower); 57; 78R (lower); 96 lower; 101R, top, middle and lower; 134L and top R; 135; 136L top and lower, R (lower); 138L (top) and R (top and lower); 139; 140L and top R; 141; 142. Michael Leonard: 8R. Don Felton: 136R (top); 137L (lower). Margaret Reid: 134 R (lower). JMC Productions: 134R (top), 140L (lower). Louise Fischer Cozzi: 38L (lower), 136R (lower), 138R (lower). Rezny M.S. Photography, Inc., 141R (top). Norman Watkins: 137L (top) and R.

Library of Congress Cataloging-in-Publication Data

McMillan, Dotty.
    Creative ways with polymer clay / Dotty McMillan.
        p. cm.
      Includes index.
      ISBN 0-8069-1745-8
      1. Polymer clay craft. I. Title.
    TT297 .M42 2001
    731.4'2—dc21

                         2001020623

14 13 12 11

First paperback edition published in 2002 by
Sterling Publishing Co., Inc.
387 Park Avenue South, New York, N.Y. 10016
© 2001 by Dotty McMillan
Distributed in Canada by Sterling Publishing
c/o Canadian Manda Group, 165 Dufferin Street,
Toronto, Ontario, Canada M6K 3H6
Distributed in the United Kingdom by GMC Distribution Services,
Castle Place, 166 High Street, Lewes, East Sussex, England BN7 1XU
Distributed in Great Britain by Chrysalis Books Group PLC,
The Chrysalis Building, Bramley Road, London W10 6SP, England.
Distributed in Australia by Capricorn Link (Australia) Pty Ltd.
P.O. Box 704, Windsor, NSW 2756, Australia
Printed in China

Sterling ISBN-13: 978-0-8069-1745-0 Hardcover
ISBN-10: 0-8069-1745-8

ISBN-13: 978-1-4027-0113-9 Paperback
ISBN-10: 1-4027-0113-6

For information about custom editions, special sales, premium and corporate purchases, please contact Sterling Special Sales Department at 800-805-5489 or specialsales@sterlingpub.com.

Contents

Tools
Supplies &
Basic
Information

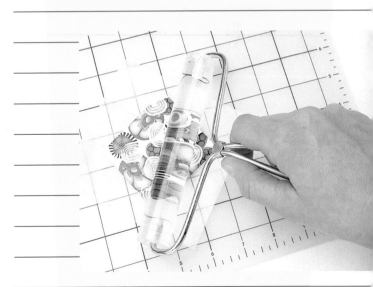

A LITTLE HISTORY

Polymer clay is the art medium that has set the imagination of hundreds of artists on fire since 1991. Why? Because polymer clay has far more potential for diversity than any other art medium. Once you start working with it, you'll quickly discover its unique and amazing qualities.

Polymer clay is fairly new on the art scene, compared to mediums such as earth clays, oil paints, wood, and precious metals. It was born in the era when plastics were being developed. An early plastic called Bakelite, developed by Belgian chemist Dr. Leo H. Baekeland in 1907, started the craze for all things plastic. Polymer clay is one of the "after Bakelite" plastics, and owes its existence to Bakelite.

In the latter part of the 1930s, a woman in Germany by the name of "Fifi" Rehbinder was looking for the necessary materials to make doll heads. During her experiments, she discovered a clay-like byproduct and named it *Fifi Mosaik* after her nickname. Since the "clay" was usable for many other projects, and was easily hardened in her home oven, she decided that other people would

enjoy using it also. She began her own business, marketing the clay, and did so until 1964, when she went to the German company Eberhard Faber with it. At that time, the product we now know as FIMO™ polymer clay was born. Later, several other companies began to manufacture their own brands of polymer clay. Today, the clay is available in a variety of brands, each with its own unique characteristics, and in a rainbow of colors.

In the early '90s, Nan Roche introduced this remarkable art medium to the world via her book *The New Clay*. Nan displayed the clay's creative potential in great detail with help from a number of early polymer clay pioneers. Her book sent a dynamic jolt through the art world. Artists everywhere began discovering the exciting possibilities of this relatively new substance.

Not only is polymer clay available in a glorious array of colors, you'll find it surprisingly easy to work with. Mold and shape it by hand, or use all sorts of everyday items to form and texture it. Discover how to make faux jade, turquoise, ivory, wood, and polished or aged metal. Bundle rods of color together to form colorful millefiori pattern canes. Applique, stamp, carve, saw, sand, and buff it. Mix in a variety of inclusions, such as spices from the kitchen, for wonderfully unique effects. Use the clay for painting pictures or forming mosaics; shape it into lamps, vessels, boxes, and purses; or turn it into buttons, beads, and beautiful baubles. What more could an artist or crafter possibly want?

Canework by Sylvia Schmahmann.

WHAT IS POLYMER CLAY?

Polymer clay is a smooth, relatively soft claylike plastic that is easily coaxed into just about any shape; it can then be hardened in a home oven and turned into a stable and durable object.

Unlike natural clay from the earth, polymer clay was developed in a chemist's laboratory. It is made from polyvinyl chloride (PVC), which is used to make such things as plumbing pipes, mixed with plasticizers and color pigments. It is a thermosetting plastic, which means that it is set into a solid form by the action of heat, after which it can't be reformed. When polymer clay is baked at a temperature range of from 212°F to

275°F (100°C to 135°C), it undergoes chemical changes. The particles fuse into a solid shape, and the shape is retained.

Polymer clay comes in various kinds and colors, including: opaque colors, translucent colors, colorless translucent, liquid translucent, liquid opaque white, a form that remains flexible and stretchy after baking, stone and granite types, and a form that absorbs light and glows in the dark (Photo 1).

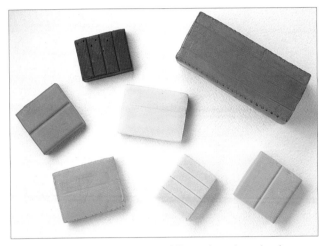

1. Polymer clay comes in many different brands and colors.

SAFETY CONCERNS

Some basic safety rules should be followed when using any art medium. This is true for polymer clay also. Your tools and equipment should be reserved for working with polymer clay and never used for food, because the plasticizer, which makes the clay malleable, is hazardous if eaten.

Like most plastics, if it is overheated, polymer clay will turn dark, or burn and give off noxious fumes. Be careful not to burn the clay or overheat the clay, as the fumes and cinders it will emit should not be inhaled. It's important to use an oven thermometer for an accurate reading of how hot your oven is, to avoid burning. If something burns, air out the room and leave the room until the fumes have gone.

The clay can be baked in your home oven if you are doing only small amounts of work. Because the fumes of burnt clay are toxic, if you do a considerable amount, it would be wise to invest in a toaster oven or a convec-tion oven that is used only for the clay. If possible, set it up outside the home, in a garage, patio, etc. Then if your polymer clay burns, the fumes will be away from your main living/eating area, and cleanup will be easier. **Caution:** Never put polymer clay in the microwave, or under a direct flame.

When sanding the clay, use wet/dry sandpaper with water so that the polymer dust isn't inhaled or spread around to possibly contaminate food. Wear a mask when working with powdered metals or mica. If your skin appears to be sensitive to the unbaked clay, wear thin, tight Latex gloves while working with it. When buffing your items on a buffing wheel, wear a face mask, as painters do, to avoid inhaling the residue (Photo 2).

After using polymer clay, wash your hands carefully; you can use baby wipes, baby oil, or isopropyl alcohol, followed by soap and water.

Polymer clay should not be used by children under 5, who might eat it. Play dough made from flour, salt, and food coloring can be used for young children instead.

These are easy-to-follow rules that should relieve you of any safety concerns you might have concerning polymer clay.

2. Face masks are important for work with powdered items, such as mica and powdered metals. Rubber gloves are used by some people to protect their hands, if they are allergic to the chemicals in polymer clay.

TOOLS AND EQUIPMENT

If you are just beginning to work with polymer clay, you'll find you can achieve a great deal even with basic tools. Here are some suggested items to get you started.

3. A number of helpful clay tools. Top: Drill, carving tool, cutting blade, needle, clay tool. Top right: Pasta machine. Middle: Dremel® tool, with attachments. Front: Brayers, cutting blades, grater, and shaping tools.

1. Work surface: A tile, heavy piece of glass, Plexiglas™, or other smooth sturdy surface.

2. A sharp blade: Tissue blades or other sharp steel blades are recommended, but to begin with an industrial razor blade or sharp craft knife will suffice.

3. Roller: Choose one made of Plexiglas or marble, or any roller that has an extremely smooth surface.

4. Oven: Your regular home oven is alright if you are not going to do a great many pieces. Get a toaster oven or a convection oven and reserve it for clay use if you are going to do a lot of work.

5. Polymer clay: See page 14 for the different kinds available. Each project lists the kinds you will need for that project.

6. Liquid translucent polymer clay: For creating unusual effects on the clay; also used as an aid when attaching unbaked clay to baked clay (Photo 4).

4. Sculpey diluent and Liquid Sculpey clay.

7. Oven thermometer: For checking to make sure your oven temperature is correct. This is crucial, as the dial temperatures on ovens usually are inaccurate (Photo 5).

5. A portable oven thermometer is crucial to insure that your oven's temperature is correct for baking the clay.

8. Baking surface: This could be a paper-covered metal or heatproof glass pan or sheet, or ceramic tile.

9. Needle or needle tool: For making holes in beads.

10. Pasta machine: This is optional. You can manage without it, but you'll be glad if you get one. Used for rolling out smooth, even sheets of clay in various thicknesses and for conditioning the clay and mixing colors. Should not be used for food.

11. Steel ruler: Helps when cutting straight lines or measuring canes. One with millimeters on it would be helpful.

12. Variety of objects, such as carved buttons, Phillips screwdriver, thick-toothed comb, rough tree bark, etc.: To either texture the surface of unbaked clay, or to penetrate deeply into the clay for certain techniques.

13. Fire extinguisher: A handy thing to have around, in the rare event that your clay catches fire.

14. Buffing wheel or buffing cloth: For bringing up a shine on the surface of the clay.

15. Sandpaper: Wet/dry sandpaper in various grits from 220 to 2000 grit, including 320, 400 and 600 for smoothing the surface of baked clay, or rounding off or smoothing rough edges. Sanding wet minimizes the amount of dust in the air, which is healthier.

16. Mold release: For example, talc, cornstarch, or Armorall™.

17. Dust mask: To wear while buffing or working with powders.

18. Safety glasses: To wear while buffing or sanding.

19. Parchment paper, tracing paper, or bakery paper: To make lifting and turning pieces of clay easier, for baking in oven, tracing, etc.

20. Aluminum foil: For shaping interiors of various forms to reduce the weight.

With these few items, you can get to know the clay and be able to do a great many exciting projects. However, if you want to jump headfirst into the work, or have been working with polymer clay already for some time, here is a list of other tools for you to choose from. You certainly don't need every item on this list, so don't be intimidated. Many tools can be improvised from things you have at home.

1. A mini-food processor: If you are using one of the harder clays, such as FIMO™ Classic, this is an excellent way to start the conditioning.

2. Brayer: A smaller version of the roller.

3. Dremel™ tool: For drilling holes or buffing, using a buffing attachment (Photo 6).

6. Dremel tool and wet/dry sandpaper. A wide variety of attachments can be added to the Dremel tool, including sanding and buffing attachments.

4. Extruder: To press out various shapes of clay or long, stringlike pieces.

5. Noodle cutter: For cutting long, even strips of clay.

6. Cookie cutters and small aspic cutters: For cutting various shapes (Photo 7).

7. Dental tools: For modeling and sculpting.

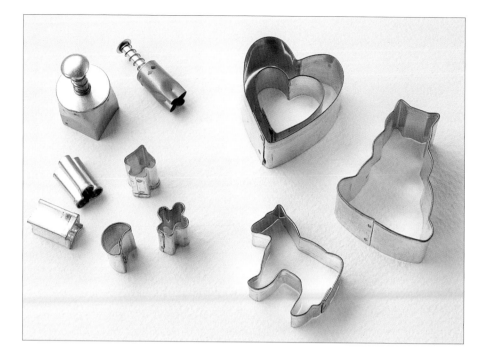

7. A wide variety of cutters comes in handy. Top, Kemper tool; left bottom, aspic cutters; right, cookie cutters.

8. Rubber stamps: For texturing the surface of the clay and for creating images on the surface of the clay. You can make stamps yourself (see Rubber Stamps section of book).

9. Molds and rubber stamp molds: For easy shaping of the clay (Photo 8).

10. Wood-carving tools: For carving and incising baked pieces of clay.

11. Clay modeling tools: For sculpting.

12. Metallic foils: Real or imitation gold, silver, or copper foils. To use as adornment on the clay surface or under the surface (Photo 9). The imitation ones are used by most people as they are much less expensive.

13. Acrylic paints: For antiquing baked clay. Burnt sienna and burnt umber are popular for this purpose.

14. Metallic or mica powders and embossing powders:

8. Molds, stamps, and colored pencils are all useful tools for working with polymer clay.

9. Imitation gold leaf is used for mokume gane and other techniques.

To use on or in unbaked clay to produce a colorful sheen or metallic effect.

15. Inclusions such as dried herbs, colored sand, or tiny beads (Photos 10 and 11).

16. A color wheel: An aid in mixing and combining colors of clay.

17. Bead supports: Wooden skewers, wire, or knitting needles to hold beads when baking.

18. Paintbrushes: For antiquing, glazing, painting, and applying powders.

19. Colored pencils: For coloring black-and-white transfers.

20. Mineral oil or diluent (the latter is sold by the clay companies): For conditioning clay that is too hard and crumbly.

21. Scissors, regular or patterned: For trimming or edging both baked and unbaked clay.

22. Garlic press: Makes narrow strings of clay, often used for hair on small figures.

23. Leafing pens: Gold, silver, and copper pens for drawing on or highlighting baked clay.

24. Metallic wax: A rub-and-buff substance to give baked clay the appearance of metal.

25. Mini-grater: For generating tiny bits of clay.

26. Graph paper: Makes cutting and measuring easier.

27. Clay-compatible glaze or finish: Sculpey glaze, FIMO glaze, Flecto Diamond Varathane Elite, Future acrylic floor finish.

28. Pin vise equipped with a drill bit: To either drill holes in baked clay or to enlarge holes in baked clay.

10 and 11. Some inclusions to add to or on unbaked clay: Colored sand, embossing powders, tiny beads.

29. Polyester stuffing (the kind used for stuffing toys or quilts): For holding rounded objects while they bake.

30. Jewelry findings such as necklace closures, pin backs, and cords or bead wire for jewelry. See individual projects for specific ones.

31. Metal mesh: For reinforcing and shaping heavy projects.

A WORD ABOUT
THE CLAYS

Polymer clay comes in a variety of brands; each has a slightly different texture and qualities. All of the brands are excellent. Try each of them and choose the one or ones you find easiest to work with, as well as ones that result in colors and surfaces that please you. Some of the projects in this book call for specific clays; see individual projects for details. Many artists use several brands and types of clay, depending upon the projects they are working on. Below are some of the ones available.

❖ Sculpey III® (by Polyform Products Co., Elk Grove Village, Illinois) comes in a great many colors and is the softest and easiest of the polymer clays to condition. This is the weakest of the clays after baking.

❖ Premo! Sculpey® (by Polyform) was developed especially for the polymer clay artist by Polyform Products Co. and Marie Segal of The Clay Factory of Escondido, California. Premo! is medium soft and is easy to condition. It holds cane patterns well and is extremely strong and somewhat flexible after baking. It comes in a wide variety of artist's colors, which change very little or not at all after baking.

❖ FIMO™, manufactured by Eberhard Faber in Germany, is now available in a FIMO Soft version, which is much easier to condition than the original FIMO, and in FIMO Classic, which has the characteristics of the original FIMO. FIMO Classic can be difficult to condition, but holds patterns extremely well. Baking gives it a very nice matte finish. FIMO is quite strong after baking. It is a favorite of many clay artists.

❖ Cernit®, manufactured by T & F GmBH in Germany, is the strongest of the clays and develops a lovely porcelainlike surface after it is baked. It is a favorite of many dollmakers. Some of its colors are very strong, but diluting them with white gives wonderful results. Dollmakers often use a mixture of Cernit Flesh color and Super Sculpey clay, which is beige toned, for a very workable and attractive finish.

❖ Friendly Plastic® modeling material is manufactured by AMACO®, American Clay Company, of Indianapolis, Indiana. A fairly strong clay after baking, Friendly has a nice matte finish. It is somewhat difficult to condition, but holds patterns quite well.

❖ Super Sculpey® (Polyform Products Co.). This is a very strong beige-toned clay that comes in large blocks. It can be used for figures that are going to be painted, as a base to which you may apply cane slices or other decorations, or mixed with Cernit or other flesh-colored clay for dollmaking.

❖ Sculpey® SuperFlex (Polyform Products Co.) is an extremely soft clay to work with and remains quite flexible after baking. It is especially good for making molds with undercuts.

❖ Translucent Liquid Sculpey® (Polyform Products Co.) is a liquid form of polymer clay that can be used as a surface enhancement, as an aid to help adhere baked and unbaked pieces together during the second baking, and as a transfer medium. It can be colored with oil paint, pigments, mica powders, and embossing powders.

Note: Although some clay manufacturers tell you that you must not mix the different brands of clay together, many clay artists have been doing just that for many years with no adverse results. Mixing a soft brand of clay with a hard brand is one way of making a more workable medium. Intermixing can create many different and unusual colors. Keep notes so that you can repeat the results.

PREPARING THE CLAY

In order to have strength and stability, polymer clay must be conditioned before it is used. This is necessary even if the clay you choose is nice and soft and workable. Nowadays, conditioning is not difficult and should not take much time. Before the discovery that a mini-food processor and a pasta machine made this job quite easy, most artists conditioned clay completely by hand. You can still do this job by hand if you prefer, or if the expense of the machines is too much for your budget.

Conditioning by hand: Warm the clay before beginning. Placing a packet of clay next to your body warmth—under your arm, or in the waistband of your skirt or slacks—will do the trick. An alternative is to set it on a bun warmer or heating pad. Don't overdo the warming, or your clay will begin to bake. Work only small pieces of the clay at a time. Roll the clay out into a long snake, fold it in half, twist it together, roll into a ball, and repeat this process a number of times, until the clay is smooth and workable (Photos 12 and 13).

Conditioning by machine may only require that you use a pasta machine, depending on which clay you are using. For a clay that is not hard and crumbly, you need to run it through the pasta machine on the thickest setting, fold it in half, and run it through again, folded end first (Photo 14). Repeat this process 5 to 10 times, until clay is smooth and workable. If the clay is hard and crumbly, cut it into small chunks and drop it into a mini-food processor and run the processor for about 25 seconds, or until the clay is warm and has turned into tiny balls. If the clay feels very dry, add one or two drops of mineral oil or one of the additives put out by the clay companies for this purpose (Sculpey diluent or Quick-Mix by FIMO). Don't add too much to begin with, as you can easily make your clay way too soft and sticky. Remove the clay from the processor and press it into a patty that is thin enough to go through the thickest setting on the pasta machine. Roll and fold the clay through the machine 5 to 10 times. Your clay will now be well-conditioned and ready to use.

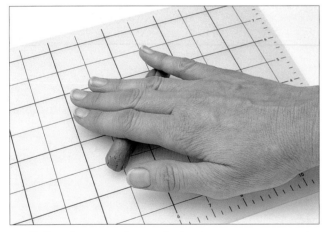

12. Rolling clay to condition it by hand.

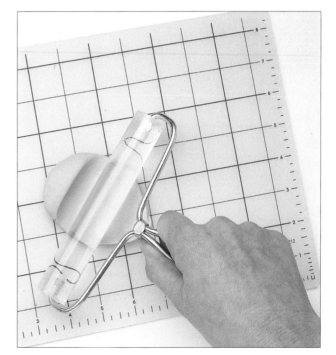

13. An acrylic brayer or roller is helpful in rolling out the clay.

14. A pasta machine may be used to condition clay, to roll it to a uniform thickness, and for other things.

SOME MEASUREMENTS

Many projects suggest using a pasta machine for rolling sheets of clay to a desired thickness. If you don't have a pasta machine, this can be done with your hands and an acrylic or marble rolling pin or printer's brayer, using a ruler to check the thicknesses of the sheets. The settings on pasta machines aren't standard-ized, so if you use one, do some tests to see what thickness you get on each setting of your machine, and make a little setting chart for yourself if the thicknesses are different from those in the chart given here, which is based on the author's Atlas pasta machine. We will use settings and thicknesses throughout the book, so even if your settings are different, you will know what thickness of clay to roll.

Pasta Machine Settings*

Settings	Inches	mm
#1	⅛	3.2
#2	⁷⁄₆₄	2.8
#3	³⁄₃₂	2.4
#4	⁵⁄₆₄	2
#5	¹⁄₁₆	1.6
#6	¹⁄₃₂	0.8
#7	¹⁄₄₀	0.6

*Based on the author's pasta machine.

BAKING THE CLAY

Manufacturers of polymer clays include guidelines with the clays on how hot to bake them. The goal is to get the small polymer clay particles hot enough to fuse together, but not so hot that they burn. Thin objects get heated through faster than thick ones. Thick objects may burn on the outside but not be fused on the inside if the temperature is too high. Different clays have different recommended baking times and temperatures, and with some brands, such as FIMO, translucents have different recommended baking temperatures than colors.

Here are several things to keep in mind:

1. Use an oven thermometer, rather than relying on the oven dial's calibrations, which frequently are inaccurate. Each oven is slightly different from the others.

An increase of even 25°F can be the difference between baking well and overbaking (turning brown) or underbaking.

2. Preheat the oven to the correct temperature before inserting your pieces, unless a project specifically suggests you use a cool oven.

3. Bake your clay pieces on a surface that doesn't conduct heat well, such as a ceramic tile, parchment paper, or card stock, or use an ovenproof dish that is reserved for clay only (not used for food). Don't place the pieces too close to the heating element.

4. For each new clay you use, bake a few sample squares at various temperatures and thicknesses, to see what temperature you need to use at the thickness you are planning. Label and save these squares for reference.

5. Transparent and flesh tones of FIMO and Sculpey need to be baked at a lower temperature (212°F, 100°C) than the other colors. When you add one-fourth or more FIMO translucent or Sculpey III translucent to a color, you should use the translucent temperature recommended by the manufacturer. However, if you add less than that, it's best to bake at the temperature recommended for the colored clay. Otherwise the colored clay won't be properly cured.

6. Don't bake polymer clay in a microwave oven or under a broiler.

7. In the event of a fire, put out the fire with a fire extinguisher or baking soda, open the windows to get rid of the fumes, and leave the room until the fumes have cleared.

Some Basic Techniques

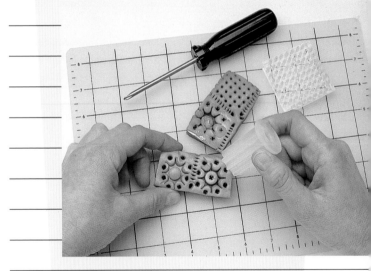

In order to avoid repeating the instructions for certain techniques over and over again with each project, I have put many of them into the following section so that you can refer to them whenever you need to. In some projects, however, you will find less common or even brand-new techniques, which will be explained while you are in the process of doing those projects.

1 IMAGE TRANSFERS

Black-and-White Transfers

One of the intriguing things about polymer clay is its ability to grab different types of images and hold on to them. You or your children may have played with some clay or some Silly Putty™ modeling clay and set it down on a newspaper, only to find later that it had picked up an image from the paper. Polymer clay will do the same thing.

Black-and-white transfers are best done using a copy-shop copy made on a machine that uses toner. They can also be done with a copy from a laser printer copy that uses toner. (You can even use a black pencil, but the outlines won't be as crisp, and the copy must be weighted when baking.) For the best image, always use a fairly fresh copy. After a month or so, the toner seems to degrade or harden, and your image will not be as good as it should be, or it may not transfer at all. Many other methods of doing black-and-white transfers have been developed. I prefer the fast and easy method that I call my 5-minute transfer technique, given below. I've found it almost fail-safe:

1. Prepare a piece of clay of the size and shape you want. This should be a smooth, flat, light-colored or white piece of clay (Photo 1).

2. Lay the clay on whatever baking surface you will be using. This step is very important.

3. Cut out your transfer picture from its paper and lay it face down on the clay surface.

4. Burnish the back of the paper well. Rub the paper with a smooth, hard object such as a bone folder, paper-embossing burnishing tool, a tongue depressor, or the dull edge of a dinner knife. Rub hard enough to assure that the paper is well seated on the clay, but not so hard that you dig into the clay. Burnish the surface three or four times (Photo 2).

5. Place the clay on its baking surface in a preheated oven. Use an oven thermometer to get exactly the temperature that has been recommended by the clay manufacturer. DO NOT pick up the clay from the baking surface, as this can dislodge the paper. Any area that the paper does not touch during baking will not transfer.

6. Bake the piece for 5 minutes. Remove the piece from the oven and slowly and carefully lift off the paper (Photo 3). Return the clay to the oven and continue baking for the rest of the required time for that kind/thickness of clay.

This method is fast and easy. It should give you a nice sharp, dark transfer, as long as your paper copy is fresh and is well adhered to the clay.

1. A laser print of a picture, a burnisher, and white clay.

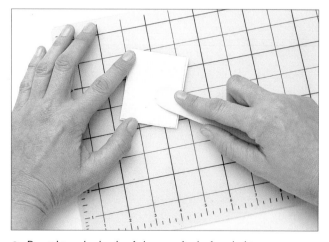

2. Burnishing the back of the transfer before baking to assure a good transfer.

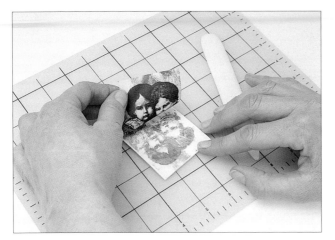

3. Lifting transfer on clay after baking. Image is reversed.

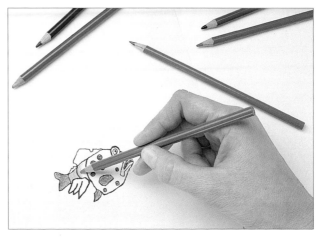

1. A black-and-white transfer can be colored with colored pencils.

This Music Pin was made with black-and-white transfers.

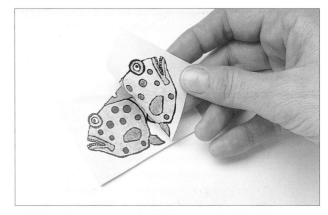

2. Lifting the paper reveals the heat-transferred image.

Black-and-White Transfers with Colored Pencils

This technique is exactly the same as the regular black-and-white transfer, except for one step. Before cutting out your black-and-white image, color it with colored pencils (Photo 1). Make sure that you exert enough pressure to coat the paper well with the color, so that it will transfer well. Different brands of colored pencils and certain colors create different effects (Photo 2). It is wise to do some testing before you begin a project so that you won't be disappointed in the results.

Pin made with black-and-white transfer colored with colored pencils.

Color Transfers

There are two types of color transfers: ones that are done with copy shop color copies and ones that are done with inkjet T-shirt transfer copies.

Color copies of pictures that are done at a copy shop will transfer onto the clay via the same method used for the regular black-and-white transfers (see above). However, the image with this type of transfer is often light or pale, although now and then you may get a brighter image, depending on where you have your copy made. Try different copy shops until you find one whose color copies transfer well. (Softer, paler images may be just the effect you want, however.)

Color transfers made with T-shirt transfer paper.

For really bright, color-true transfers, you must use inkjet T-shirt transfer paper manufactured by Canon or Hewlett Packard. These are the only two that I know of at this time that work well. This method is more complicated than the other transfer methods, but well worth doing. First of all you will need a computer, a paint or picture editing program, and an inkjet printer. If you plan to use photographs or other pictures besides the ones you have on your computer, you will also need access to a scanner.

Once you have your image printed out on the T-shirt transfer paper, you are ready to go. Follow all of the directions for the black-and-white transfers, with the ex-

ception of the timing. Bake the color transfer for 7 to 10 minutes before removing the piece from the oven, and then very carefully peel off the paper. Return the piece to the oven and complete the baking time. The transfer paper works because it is coated with a gluelike substance, which melts onto the clay.

Sometimes you will notice some waviness or tiny bumps on the surface after the piece is baked. This can't always be avoided. However, you can coat the surface with a very thin layer of Translucent Liquid Sculpey and rebake it. Be sure you coat all the way to the edge of the piece and then on around onto the side edges. Otherwise the liquid clay will tend to peel off. The baked surface can then be sanded and buffed, or left as is. Glazing is also a possibility, using two or more coats of any of the clay-compatible glazes. Or buff surface with 000 steel wool for a matte finish.

Translucent Liquid Sculpey Transfers

Another method of doing color transfers is to use liquid clay as an adjunct. There are some colored magazine pictures that will transfer using the liquid. Once you use the picture, that's it; you can't use it again. Coat a piece of glass or nonporous tile with Translucent Liquid Sculpey. Cut out the picture and lay it face down on the Translucent Sculpey. Bake with the paper in place. Carefully peel off the paper; your image will have been transferred onto the clay.

Images that have been printed with an inkjet printer onto T-shirt transfer paper can also be transferred in this way. A very thin layer of Translucent Liquid Sculpey applied to the clay is also helpful to speed up the transfer of black-and-white images and to urge older copies to transfer.

Translucent Liquid Sculpey clay.

RUBBER STAMPS, CLAY STAMPS, AND MOLDS

Rubber stamps are great tools to use with clay. However, not all rubber stamps are equal. Stamps that are cut too shallow do not give much of an impression. Be sure to check how deeply the rubber is cut when you buy them. What you want are nice, straight sides and edges. If they are rounded, they will not work well. Also, the harder the rubber, the better. Acrylic stamps are even better, but these usually must be custom-made (Photo 1).

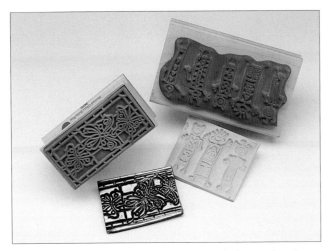

1. Rubber stamps and clay from stamps, which may then be gilded (left front) if desired.

Soft, spongy material makes for soft, diffuse impressions. Also, think about size and detail and make sure they are suited for use with the clay. Huge, bold stamps may not give you the look you want, and very finely detailed ones may not show up as much as you'd like. It won't take you long to learn which ones are the most effective.

Making Rubber Stamps

Your own art can be reborn as a rubber stamp very easily. Here's how. For this your art must be a black-and-white line drawing. If you feel you can't draw well, then check out the copyright-free graphics that come with many computer programs or are found in a variety of books. Images from these sources are often us-

able as long as they are black-and-white (no gray tones). Size them up or down to suit your needs. Copy shops can do this for you, or if you have a computer, scanner and printer, you are all set.

Another way to create "original" art for making rubber stamps is to use a collage method. (Clay artist Mari O'Dell developed this technique.) Collect a wide variety of printed images from rubber stampings, books, and other sources; then cannibalize them by cutting out portions and recombining them into your own art.

So now you have the images. How do you turn them into rubber stamps? It's easy and fairly inexpensive. First, arrange as many images as you can get inside a 9" × 7" (22 × 18 cm) space on a white piece of paper. This is your camera-ready art. Next, find one of the rubber stamp suppliers that specializes in making these types of stamps and send off your copy. As a rule, you will get back three things: a sheet of rubber stamps, which can be cut apart and mounted onto wood or baked clay; a sheet of rigid plastic that is the same as the rubber stamps, except that it tends to work better when impressing the clay; and a matrix board that is actually a mold of the rubber stamps.

How to Use Your Stamps

Before using your stamp to impress a design into the clay, spray the stamp lightly with Armorall™ (the stuff used for polishing the interior of automobiles). This acts as a release agent so that the clay doesn't stick to the rubber. Cornstarch, talc, or even plain water can be used instead.

Set the stamp on your work surface with the rubber side up, and lay the clay over it. Begin pushing down on the clay with your thumbs or palms, making certain that it goes into all of the recessed areas. Gently peel the clay away from the stamp. If you want to have designs on both sides of the clay, use another rubber stamp on top with the rubber (image) side toward the clay, and press downwards with it instead of just with your hands alone. Some clay artists stand on top of the stamp for added pressure.

There are several ways to impress the sides of beads (Photo 2). One is to make a base bead and then impress a sheet of clay and wrap that around the base bead and secure it. Another method is to hold the bead on a knit-

2. Molded faux ivory beads.

ting needle and roll it over the rubber stamp. It's difficult to get a deep impression this way without distorting the bead. For a square or rectangular bead, you can put the clay between two rubber stamps and press them together, then turn the bead and do the same on the other two pairs of sides.

After your clay is impressed, you can gild the raised areas with mica or metallic powders (see the section of the book on Gilding). After baking, you can antique them with various colors of acrylic paint to accent the image. Alternatively, you can bake the clay and lightly sand and then buff the raised areas to a bright shine. You will find many uses and techniques for your rubber stamps, so keep a good supply of them on hand.

Clay Stamps

You can also make impression tools of polymer clay. Shape the clay into the design you want, being certain the walls of the tool that will go into the raw clay are fairly thin. Bake these tools for at least an hour at the recommended temperature to assure they are sturdy. Spray all of your impression tools with Armorall or dust them with talc or cornstarch before using so they don't stick to the unbaked clay.

Molds

A number of commercial molds made just for use with polymer clay are available, including ones that have a stamp on one side and a mold of that stamp on the other (Photo 3). You can also use candy or food molds (but don't use them for food after that). Best of all, you can make molds from all sorts of objects, including rubber stamps. The impression taken from a stamp mold is different than the one taken from the stamp itself.

3. Molds can be made or purchased. In hands: Face mold and resulting face.

Molds from Found Objects. You will discover these are easy to do. Choose an object without undercuts, as these would make it impossible to remove the clay. Take scrap clay. Mix it together well, until it is all one color. Make a pad of the clay that is wide enough for the object you are going to mold and deep enough so that after it is pressed into the clay there will still be at least ¼" (0.6 cm) at the bottom. Coat the surface of the clay and the object you are going to mold with Armorall, cornstarch, talc, or another mold release. Center the object over the clay and slowly press it downward. If the sides of the clay bow out, press them back into shape. When the object is as far into the clay as you want, gently wiggle the piece a bit to loosen it, and lift it out.

Bake the mold for at least one hour to make certain it is strong. When cool, coat it with a mold release before using.

Molds from Stamps. Making a mold from a rubber stamp is done the same way as the mold just described, except that you do not need such a thick pad of clay. Set your stamp on your work surface, rubber (image) side up, and lay the pad of clay on top. Use your thumbs to press the clay down, around, and into the stamp. Go over it several times to make sure you haven't missed anything. Turn the piece over with the clay touching your work surface and press the stamp down against your work surface. Gently peel the stamp away from the clay and bake.

4a and b. Molded or stamped textures can be enhanced by gilding.

3 THE SKINNER BLEND

I was fortunate enough to be at The Clay Factory in Escondido, California, when polymer clay artist Judith Skinner was busy mixing and blending all sorts of colors of what was then a brand new polymer clay. She began laying out beautiful sheets of clay, which started with one color on one side and then blended into a second color on the other. I couldn't believe my eyes! She was easily doing something that most of us had done in a zillion tedious steps. She was developing a fantastic and innovative new technique, later named the Skinner blend after its creator.

Making a sheet of clay that has one color blending into another color is a wonderful technique that can greatly enhance many projects. You will find dozens of uses for it, and you will be amazed and excited by the results.

First, consider the colors. Some colors blend beautifully, some don't. If you incorporate clays that have all three primaries (red, yellow, and blue), the blended color in the center of the sheet of clay sometimes becomes muddy. However, at other times the result can be incredibly beautiful. Keep a record of what colors you use so that you can repeat the effect later on. Beautiful shaded blends can always be made using just one color with white. Instead of white, you might try metallic silver or ecru/beige, which will mute the main color and give it a much different look from the original. It's possible to blend more than just two colors, and you can even achieve a beautiful rainbow effect. Experiment and keep notes and swatches of what you have done. Note: Don't feel you always have to blend opaque colors. Translucent colors make lovely blends also, as do the "pearl" colors that are available.

Once you have decided on the colors, roll out a rectangular sheet of each one on the #1 (⅛" or 3.2 mm) setting of the pasta machine. These sheets should be just as wide as the pasta machine. Cut each sheet diagonally into 2 triangles. Stack the like colored triangles together — for example, white on white and black on black. Each double-thick triangle will become one-half of a rectangle (Photo 1). Fit the two different-colored triangles back into a rectangle, butting the edges together firmly. Fold the rectangle in half, from the bot-

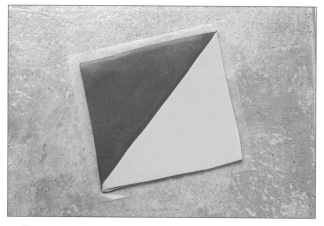

1. The start of a Skinner blend. Put two triangles of different colors of clay together to form a square or other rectangle.

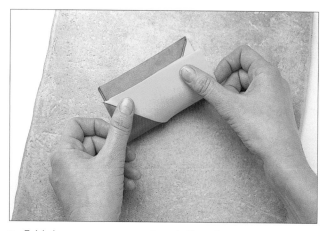

2. Fold the square or rectangle in half as shown.

tom up (Photo 2). Place the folded edge into the pasta machine and run it through on the thickest setting (Photo 3). Fold the rectangle again, exactly the same way as you did before, from the bottom up. Do not change directions and fold from another side, as this will ruin your blend. Run the clay through the pasta machine again. Continue doing this for approximately 20 times, or until the color blend is nice and smooth (Photo 4).

Now you can turn your sheet sideways and run it through the pasta machine on the second-thickest setting ($\frac{7}{64}$" or 2.8 mm). Do not fold it. If the piece is too wide across when turned this way to fit in the machine, cut it down the middle and stack the two pieces together. Roll the piece through the machine a second time on a setting that is two levels thinner, and repeat until you reach the thinnest setting that you know you can use without the clay shredding or sticking to the rollers. For some machines this will be a #5 setting ($\frac{1}{16}$" or 1.6 mm). For others it may be a #6 or #7 ($\frac{1}{32}$" or $\frac{1}{40}$"; 0.8 or 0.6 mm). Some machines have the widths numbered in reverse, so do what will achieve the desired thickness on your particular machine. You will end up with a very long and very thin sheet of clay that should blend from one color at one end to the second color at the other end.

Now you have some choices. You can roll this long sheet into a log (to make a blended cane), starting at either end of the sheet. Or fold the long sheet back and

3. Run the folded piece through the pasta machine, with folded end fed in first.

4. After numerous foldings (in the same direction) and running through the machine, the blend is complete.

CREATIVE WAYS WITH POLYMER CLAY

forth, accordion style, to make a blended loaf. Try cutting and stacking pieces so that one color is at one end and the other color is at the other end. Once your log or loaf is finished, you can use it for all sorts of projects. For instance, a shaded log works very well when making the petals for flower canes. It gives an illusion of dimension.

There are several other ways to do a Skinner blend, placing the triangles differently. You will find these demonstrated on a number of polymer clay videotapes.

4 MOKUME GANE

This unusual polymer clay technique has been adapted from an ancient Japanese metalworking version. The clay is wonderfully suited for this multilayered technique. There are several ways of achieving mokume gane's lovely effects, all of which work extremely well. See which of them works best for your projects. Translucent clay and metallic leaf are the main ingredients of most but not all of the mokume gane techniques.

A number of polymer clay artists have developed their own special ways of doing this lovely technique. Many of these artists have videotapes available, which show exactly how it is done. Look on the Internet for further information. Below I have included a rundown on a number of different mokume techniques, for use in the projects in this book.

Faux etched glass beads are made with impressed from top mokume gane technique.

A Simple Crackle Mokume

This method is the fastest and easiest mokume technique. However, in exchange for the ease and speed, you will sacrifice some of the brilliance, as well as some of the traditional traits of other mokume gane techniques.

Roll out a sheet of translucent clay on the #5 setting (1⁄16" or 1.6 mm) of the pasta machine. Smooth it out on your work surface and then lay a sheet of gold, silver, or copper leaf on top and smooth it carefully. (You might wish to use some of each of these leaves for a lovely effect.) Lift the sheet of clay and run it back through the pasta machine on a #6 (1⁄32" or 0.8 mm) setting. This will crackle the metallic leaf.

Lay this sheet (leaf side down) onto whatever base you choose, such as that for a bead, a pin, or pendant. (You put the leaf side down because you want the foil under a thin sheet of translucent, which protects it and gives it the look of being deep in the clay.) Trim it to the size you want on the base. Be careful of the color of the base, as it will show through wherever there is no metallic leaf. Smooth the clay from the center out to avoid bubbles. Bake and, while still hot, plunge the piece into ice water and let cool. Plunging a hot baked piece of mokume gane, or any piece that is made with translucent clay, into ice water to cool helps clarify and make the surface more transparent. Sand and buff the surface to a high shine.

Tip: When you are tinting translucent clay, start with just a tiny piece of the color and add more as needed.

Topographical Mokume*

Roll out a number of balls of translucent clay about the size of a walnut. Tint each ball a different color or shade with your choice of opaque clay. Add only a tiny amount of the opaque color to the translucent. Flatten each ball and run it through the pasta machine on the #4 or #5 setting (5⁄64" or 1⁄16", 2 or 1.6 mm). You want each sheet to be quite thin. Cut the sheets into squares about 3" × 3" (7.5 × 7.5 cm).

*The topographical mokume technique was developed by Lindly Haunani.

Layer as follows: Lay down a translucent sheet of clay, then a sheet of gold leaf (or other color) on top of it, then a translucent sheet of clay. Repeat until you have a stack that is about 1½ to 2" (4 to 5 cm) tall.

Roll out 6 to 8 balls of tinted translucent clay a little larger than peas. Turn over the pad of stacked clay and metallic leaf, and place the balls randomly over the bottom surface of the pad. Leave some space between each of them (Photo 1). Press them lightly to adhere them to the surface. Turn the pad over and set it on your work surface. Press down around each of the balls of clay. Do not press the balls themselves, just the spaces between them. Your finished result should look somewhat like a 3-D topographical map.

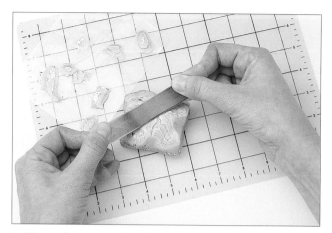

2. The pad is set upright and very thin slices are taken across it.

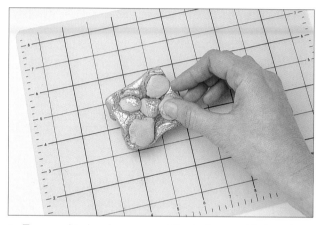

1. Topographical mokume gane. Clay balls are added to the back of the pad.

Press your mokume pad against the work surface to anchor it somewhat so that when you are taking slices from it, it won't move. Using a very sharp, thin blade held horizontally with the sharp edge toward you, take extremely thin slices from the tops or domes of clay on your topographical pad. Lay these slices on a piece of waxed paper. Take as many slices as your stack of clay will allow (Photo 2). Use your mokume gane slices for a wide variety of projects. The leftover portion of your pad can also be used, perhaps for a pin and earrings.

Impressed from the Top Mokume*

This method starts out exactly the same as the topographical version, as far as making the layers goes, although you may want to add a layer of opaque clay here and there in your stack. (Don't add the balls of clay below, however.) Once your stack is completed, begin looking around the house and/or hardware store for various items that you can use to press into the clay. These impressions will be made into the top surface of the stack. Some things that work fairly well are: a large Phillips screwdriver, a zigzag blade, plastic protectors for the bottoms of narrow-legged chairs, a dinner knife to make Xs or squares with, and a corkscrew laid on its side (Photo 1).

*The impressed from the top mokume technique was developed by Tory Hughes.

1. Household items can be used for impressing mokume gane from the top.

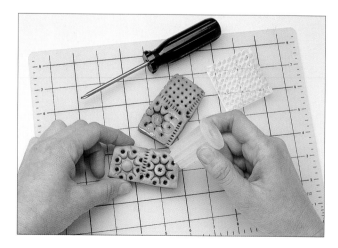

CREATIVE WAYS WITH POLYMER CLAY

Once you have completed impressing the clay, secure it to your work surface, and begin taking the same thin slices from the stacked pad as you did with the topographical pad. Set the slices aside to use on clay projects.

A Variation on the Above: Lay on a piece of black or another color of clay as the top layer. When the clay is impressed from above, the black clay will move downward for several layers, outlining the impression images. Black makes the most visible outlines, but other colors can also be used (Photo 2).

2. Variation of impressed from the top mokume gane uses black clay on top.

Jelly Roll Mokume*

Make a Skinner blend (see instructions in Skinner Blend section) of tinted translucents and roll the blend out on a #5 setting (1⁄16" or 1.6 mm) of the pasta machine. This will result in a long, thin sheet of shaded clay. Lay this sheet down on your work surface and cover it with sheets of gold, silver, copper, or multicolored metallic leaf. Press down on the metallic leaf with your fingertips in order to lightly crackle it (Photo 1). Starting at one end of the sheet, begin to roll it up, making certain that there is no air trapped. Roll slowly and smoothly, pressing the ends inward as you do (Photo 2).

Once you have your jelly roll of clay and metal leaf, you are ready to make your slices. It's best to let the roll

The jelly roll mokume technique was developed by Donna Kato.

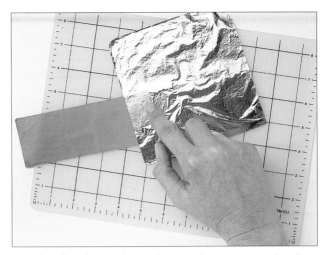

1. Jelly roll mokume. A tinted sheet of clay is covered with metallic leaf.

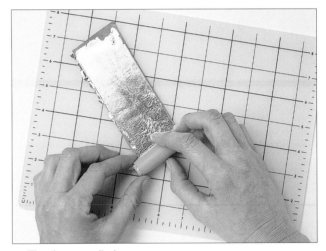

2. The sheet is rolled up into a cane.

sit for at least an hour in order to somewhat firm up. A few minutes in a freezer will help with this. Left overnight, or for several days, the roll will be even easier to slice. The mokume slices are not cut straight up and down as you would cut regular cane slices. Instead, you will make them at about a 45-degree angle to the layers, which will help to show off the metallic leaf. Take thin slices and set them aside for your project (Photo 3).

An alternative to taking very thin slices is to take a slice that is about 1⁄8" (3.2 mm) thick and run it through the pasta machine on a #5 or #6 setting (1⁄16 or 1⁄32", or 1.6 or 0.8 mm). This will thin and elongate the slice, which can then be used to cover the base clay.

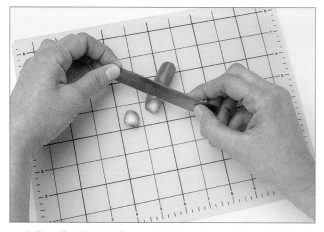

3. Jelly roll mokume. Slices are taken from the cane at a slight angle.

Impressed Slice-Off Mokume*

This is actually the reverse of most of the other methods. Instead of taking slices and using the slices to lay onto your base clay, in this method you impress the clay with rubber stamps and then take off very thin slices of the raised areas, which reveals the colors and pattern underneath. It is the underneath portion that you use to make pins and pendants, to cover vessels, and so forth.

Roll out sheets of clay in three different colors on the #1 setting (⅛", 3.2 mm) of the pasta machine. Stack the colors together. Roll the stack through the pasta machine just once on the #1 setting. Cut the sheet in half and stack again. Roll it through the pasta machine again on the same setting. This should give you 12 layers of the different colors of clay.

Use a rubber stamp or a mold made from a rubber stamp to make fairly deep impressions in the clay. Anchor your clay to your work surface so that it doesn't slip or slide when you are slicing. Using a tissue blade or other very sharp and flexible blade, begin taking extremely thin slices off the top of the raised surfaces. Be careful not to cut too deep as you will eradicate your pattern. As you slice, you will begin to see the pattern and colors that emerge from under the top layer of clay. The resulting piece can then be used for many different projects. This form of mokume looks beautiful when lightly sanded and buffed.

*The impressed slice-off mokume technique was developed by Nan Roche.

More Mokume Gane Tips

You can cover a baked piece of clay with mokume slices if you first coat the baked piece with Sobo glue or another good white glue and let it dry. Then add the slices and bake. This will help to bond the pieces together. Another method is to brush on a very thin coating of liquid clay before adding the mokume slices.

5 MAKING CANES

Cane Basics

Polymer clay has the remarkable ability to be assembled into colorful canes, which can be reduced in size and extruded, and then sliced (Photo 1). The cane does not lose the pattern that has been built into it, and each slice has the same pattern on both sides. The process is basically the making of a 3-dimensional design whose cross-section forms an image or pattern. The resulting cane has the same pattern in each cross-sectional slice. There are really only three substances with which you can make highly detailed canes. These are glass, candy, and polymer clay. Cane work is often referred to as *millefiori,* or "a thousand flowers," a concept derived from Italian glasswork, as well as from glass done in ancient Egypt. It is this remarkable ability to be caned, reduced, and extruded that sets polymer clay apart from most other artist's mediums.

1. A variety of cane shapes.

To build a cane, you need to make a series of logs, triangular prisms, rectangular solids, or any of a variety of other shapes and then combine them together in a bundle that forms a picture or design when seen at the edge of the cane, a design which runs the length of the cane. It can be an extremely fat bundle or a thin one. The bundle can be round or square. Other shapes can be made, but are much harder to reduce to the size you will need. See Photos 2 through 6 for the steps in making a round cane.

The term "reduce" means that the cane is rolled, pressed, squeezed, and stretched so that it becomes smaller across and longer. It is possible to reduce a cane that starts out with the diameter of a dinner plate all the way down to the diameter of a tiny button and still have whatever pattern you have built into it visible. I do not, however, recommend starting out with a dinner plate

4. The bundle or cane is reduced by squeezing and tugging, elongating and narrowing the cane.

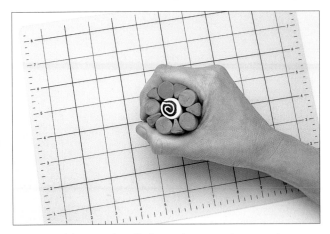

2. Colored logs are bundled together around a central core.

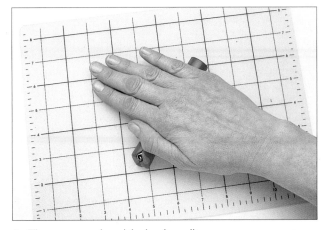

5. The cane is reduced further by rolling.

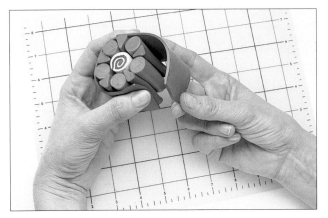

3. The bundled logs may be wrapped with a thin layer of another color of clay.

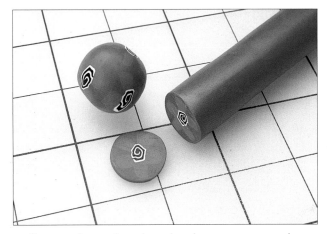

6. Slices can be cut from the reduced cane to cover or decorate almost anything, such as the bead at upper left.

size! A good size to begin with is a cane the diameter of a soda can.

Note: Cane-making with Sculpey III, which is often quite soft, can be enhanced by leaching out some of its chemicals, letting the cane sit for several days after making, and/or cooling the cane before reducing it, and again before slicing.

There are thousands of designs that can be made into canes, including, but certainly not limited to, faces, people, animals, landscapes, geometric patterns, and florals.

Reducing Canes

Every clay artist has his or her own favorite way of reducing a cane. The main objective is to reduce your cane to a usable size for whatever project you are working on without distorting the pattern inside and with as little waste clay at the ends as possible.

Round Cane. One excellent way to reduce a round cane is as follows: Grasp the cane in the middle between your thumb and your other fingers. Gently squeeze, turn the cane a quarter turn, and squeeze again. After a full turn (four squeezes), move your grasp a little more toward one end of the cane and repeat the squeezing. Repeat, moving toward the opposite ends of the cane. Continue doing this back and forth, working toward each end, until your cane is down to about two-thirds of the final diameter that you want. At this point, you can begin rolling the clay with the palms and heels of your hands and tugging outward slightly as you roll. You can reduce the cane until it's very small, but it's next to impossible to make it larger again, so you may want to leave part of your cane a larger size and set it aside while you further reduce the rest of it.

Plexiglas™ method. Another technique that many people swear by uses pieces of Plexiglas on each end of a round cane. To do this, you slice off each end of the cane so that it is perfectly flat; then place a piece of Plexiglas on each end and begin the reducing. Begin the reduction in the middle of the cane, forming a barbell or hourglass and moving outward toward the ends. The Plexiglas will create suction, which will help to keep the center of the cane from pulling inward, and thus reduce the amount of cane loss.

Square or Rectangular Solid Cane. A square cane is reduced in a slightly different manner. Set the cane upright and cup it with both hands. Use the heels of your hands to press in on the sides. Turn the cane and press inward again on the next two sides. Flip the cane over, bottom side up, and repeat the pressing. Continue alternating the sides up and the pressing until your cane is too long to handle well this way. Lay the cane down and begin rolling over the sides with a brayer or an acrylic roller. Roll a side, turn the piece one turn, and roll again. Continue this until your cane is the size you desire. It helps if you pick the cane up in your hands now and then and stretch it slightly, smoothing the sides with your fingers; then continue with the rolling (Photo 7).

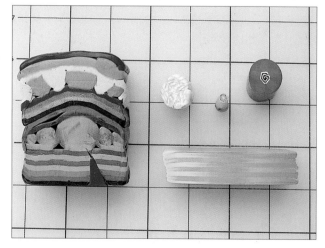

7. Canes can be made in many shapes and sizes.

Closeup of Tom Kum's Starburst Box shows a lion face cane at the bottom.

6 ANTIQUING AND CRACKLING

Antiquing

Antiquing is easy and fast. There are a number of ways to antique a piece, but the easiest way is to use acrylic paint. Two of the most popular antiquing colors are burnt umber and burnt sienna (Photo 1). However, you can antique with just about any color you wish. Using white on dark pieces is quite effective. Red on black or black on red is very dramatic.

1. Antiquing can bring out the intricacies of a molded, textured, or carved piece. Here, faux ivory before and after antiquing with acrylic paint.

When using acrylic paint for antiquing, you need a stiff brush. Load the brush with the paint and begin dabbing it onto the surface of the baked clay. The dabbing motion will help to get the paint into all the recessed areas. Continue dabbing until you have covered the entire surface of your piece. Wash your brush and put it aside. With your fingers, rub the paint around and around on the surface of the clay. When the paint starts to feel as if it is getting a little dry, use a paper towel to rub off the majority of it. It's best to wash and dry your hands then. Continue rubbing off the paint until you get the desired effect. Sometimes you may want to leave more of it on the surface; at other times you may want to have it only in the recesses. Let the remaining paint dry completely.

You can also antique with acrylic metallic paints such as copper, gold, or silver (Photo 2). These paints dry extremely quickly, so you must work fast. However, the results can be extremely pleasing as the recessed areas will hold the glint of polished metal. There are also some wonderful acrylic enhancers available, which come in either a verdigris (weathered copper) or rust finish. These have tiny bits of grit in them that will build up in areas on the surface of the clay and look much like the real thing.

2. Necklace by the author has beads that imitate antique bronze.

A second way to achieve antiquing with acrylic paints is to coat the piece with paint exactly as in the method described above, but instead of wiping off the excess paint, let all of the paint dry on the surface of the piece. When it's completely dry, use sandpaper to remove all of it except the paint in the recesses. This method works very well for impressed translucent pieces, as you can smooth and shine the surface as you remove the paint.

Chemical antiquing solutions are also available and can also be used with the clay. Since these are very strong chemicals, be certain you follow the directions exactly if you choose to use them. Work in a well-ventilated area and keep all of these solutions away from young children. Despite these drawbacks, you can achieve some wonderful effects when using commercial antiquing solutions. The clay can be made to look like copper with a thick verdigris patina as well as rusty iron, among other things. You simply paint on the metallic undercoat and, while it is still wet, go over it with a patina solution. Set the piece in a window or somewhere where there is a good airflow. Ignore it for several hours. When you come back to it, you'll be delighted with the change.

If you are using this technique on jewelry or other items that will be handled a lot, it's best to give the antiqued surface a coating of matte glaze for protection. The patina surface has a tendency to rub off with use. It is an actual patina, which is exactly the same as that formed outdoors on all copper surfaces.

Crackling

A number of crackling products are on the market today. Some work well on polymer clay; some do not. When the clay has the appearance of being crackled, it truly looks ancient (Photos 1 and 2). Try out various products and see what works for you. Most of these are two-step products. A coating of one type is applied to the clay and let dry to a certain stage. A second type of coating is then applied and let dry. With some, you can see the crackling with no trouble. With others, you will need to apply some acrylic paint that is darker than the surface of the piece, and then wipe off the excess. The paint will sink into the cracks and make them show.

Even though many of the crackling mediums say that the crackling will start immediately after applying the second solution, this doesn't always happen. If you don't see any crackling during the first half-hour or so, put the piece aside and check it the next day or several days later. You may be pleasantly surprised. On the other hand, you may not. If not, change your brand of crackle medium and try again.

1. Pendant made by the author with sage inclusions and crackled surface.

2. Closeup of same pendant.

7 GILDING TECHNIQUES

A variety of gilding methods are available to add highlights to the clay. Some of them are used on baked clay; others are applied to unbaked clay (Photo 1).

1. Supplies for gilding include gilding pens, mica powders, and waxes.

Metallic foils come in the real thing or in imitation form. The real metallic foils are quite expensive, but hold up very well and do not change color. The imitation foils are inexpensive; these are what many people use. Any foil that is on the surface of the clay needs to be coated with a clay-compatible glaze, with liquid clay, or with some other substance in order to protect it.

Mica and metallic powders come in many different colors as well as gold, silver, copper, and bronze. Be sure to use a dust mask when using these products, as metallic powders can be toxic and it is not wise to inhale mica. Powders are generally used on unbaked clay. They can be brushed on, drawn on with a clay shaper, gilded on with your fingertip, or stamped on with a rubber stamp (Photo 2). After baking, the powders need to be coated in order to protect them, using a clay-compatible glaze.

Metallic wax or leafing pen. Metallic wax is a rub-on type of product and is used after the clay is baked. It gives a soft, subtle metal look to the clay and comes in many colors, including classic gold, old gold, silver, pewter, and copper (Photo 3). Leafing pens are easy to apply to baked clay. They are much brighter than the metallic waxes and should probably be used sparingly. They come in 18K gold, silver, and copper. If you sand and buff the area on which you will be using the leafing pen, the results will be much smoother and brighter.

2. Mica powders work well for gilding raw clay.

3. Beads take on a metallic look when gilded.

8 SANDING AND BUFFING

Sanding

Not every project requires sanding and buffing, but sometimes you may want a very smooth surface and a nice shine or sheen. Sanding is actually easy to do, as long as the piece isn't too small. There is always some controversy about which grits of sandpaper to use.

Some people use just one grit of wet/dry sandpaper, while others use up to six different grits. The higher the number, the finer the grit. Some people believe you should never go below a 400-grit paper and others think it's necessary to go as high as a 2500 grit. My belief is that you should use whatever method gets the job done to your satisfaction.

Dremel tool and wet/dry sandpaper.

Wet-or-dry sandpaper (e.g., the kind used for automobiles, or carborundum paper) can be used wet and will not fall apart, an advantage in keeping dust out of your lungs.

Here is a method of sanding for those of you who want some direction. Guidelines are also given with the projects. If a piece is really lumpy, bumpy, rippled, or has rough edges you don't want, you can start with either a 220 grit or a 320 grit, and then go on to 400 and a 600 grit. If it is only a bit rough, start with a 320 grit, and progress to a 400 and then a 600. If the surface is very smooth, you can begin with a 400 grit and end with a 600. In some cases you may want to go on to a 1200, 1500, or even higher.

Sanding should not take a long time. You can only get the surface of the baked clay so smooth. If you have a lot of pieces to sand, take a bowl of water, a towel, and sit in front of the TV and watch/listen to a good old movie, or listen to talk radio. The sanding time will fly by. Sanding isn't a very intellectual activity, and your brain needs other stimulation to keep it sane.

Buffing

The results of your buffing will only be as good as your sanding. A well-sanded piece can be buffed to look like glass. Some people manage to buff their work using a small Dremel™ tool equipped with a cotton or muslin wheel. Others feel that a small jewelry buffing wheel with variable speed is best. Some prefer a full-size grinder type of machine in which the grinding wheel is replaced with a soft, one-stitch cotton or muslin wheel (this has only one line of stitching around the wheel). The latter seems to be the best choice for me. If you choose to use the Dremel tool, you need to be very careful, as it can easily dig into the clay and make an ugly trench. You could also use a cotton cloth for buffing.

If you are using a bench-type wheel, there are certain things you should be aware of. The wheel can torque a piece out of your hands and fling it across the room. If this happens, *just let it go.* Whatever you do, don't reach over or around the machine to try and stop it. Some part of you will probably be caught in the machine if you do. Torquing happens. It's a fact of buffing life. Don't let it scare you. Just go pick up your piece, dust it off, and go on with your work.

If you have long hair, tie it back before you start so it won't get caught in the equipment. This is true for using any power tools. Do not wear any jewelry that is long enough to get caught in the machinery — and no bangle type bracelets. Don't wear extremely loose or baggy clothing. Never, ever look away from the work you are doing on the machine. All sorts of things can happen if you do. If you want to look up at someone or something, pull the piece away from the wheel while you do. Wear eye protection such as safety goggles when buffing.

When you are buffing a piece, it should be held against the lower portion of the wheel (see photo). Remove the guard shield from your machine, if it has one, as it makes it impossible to buff at the correct area of the wheel. Do not stab at the wheel with the edge of a piece. It will probably get slammed out of your fingers and shot down against the floor. The piece should be held by one hand, and supported by your other. You will learn, as you practice, just how much pressure is necessary to bring up a good shine. Too much pressure can burn and blister the clay. Too little will not raise the shine.

Now that I've probably scared you out of buffing anything at all, I just want to say that once you have practiced buffing for a while, you will love doing it. You will love the look of the piece as the colors become richer. You will love the feel of the piece. It will give you a whole new perspective on working with polymer clay.

Using a bench type buffing wheel.

9 GLAZING OR SEALING

Glazing or sealing baked clay is often unnecessary. However, sometimes you will use a technique that needs a protective coating. Perhaps some foil or powders need protecting. Or maybe you do not have access to a buffing wheel and still want a nice shine. Not all materials that are made for glazing or sealing are compatible with the clay. Some will stay sticky forever.

Clay before and after glazing. Glazing enriches the colors.

Some will peel off. Most clear nail polishes are not compatible. Most spray-on glazes are not suited to polymer clay. Use products made especially for polymer clay such as the ones made for FIMO, Sculpey, and Premo! Sculpey. Alternately, you can use Flecto Diamond Varathane Elite or Future acrylic floor finish. Choose any product that dries clear, doesn't turn yellow after a time, doesn't stay tacky or become tacky after a few weeks or months, doesn't break down the surface of the clay or bubble, crack, or peel.

Glazes can be brushed on or sprayed using a non-aerosol bottle. Some items can be dipped in glaze if you are careful to avoid drips. Future floor finish is a very thin solution that can be brushed on, used as a dip, or mopped on with a piece of soft cotton T-shirt material.

10 CREATING YOUR OWN CUTTERS

You may want to cut shapes out of clay for a project. Can't find the right cookie cutter for the shape you want? Why not make your own? It's not difficult at all, but it can be a little hard on your hands. You can purchase strips of sheet metal at a hardware store in just the right size for making your own cutters. I prefer brass, which holds up extremely well over time; ¾" to 1" (2 to 2.5 cm) wide strips work just fine. Twelve-inch (30 cm) lengths give you plenty of room for most shapes, with a little left over. The only tools you will need are a sturdy pair of chain-nose pliers (for sharp bends) and small round-nose pliers (for round bends).

The first step is to decide what shape you want. Images can be drawn out by hand, created by computer, or taken from a copyright-free clip-art book. Be sure the drawings are the exact size you want for your finished cutter (enlarge or reduce the image as needed). Don't make the mistake of trying to make a very fancy shape with lots and lots of turns — at least, not to begin with. Decide where you want to start on the drawing, and mark that spot. Next, decide which direction you are going to go, to the left on the pattern or to the right. Mark an arrow on the drawing next to your starting spot, showing that direction.

Leave an inch or two (2.5 to 5 cm) of the metal strip at the beginning; then grip the strip with the pliers, making certain that they extend completely across the width of the metal. Twist the pliers in whatever direction you need in order to make your first

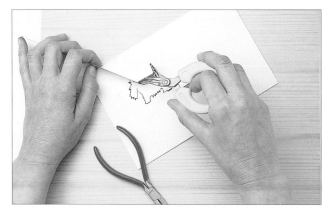

A strip of brass is bent into shape to make a cutter.

turn. Move the pliers and make the next turn. Check the size and placement of these turns against your pattern and readjust them if necessary. Don't try to hurry the process. Stay with each turn until it looks right. Continue on around the strip, making each turn as you come to it. When all of the turns are completed, hold the cutter against the pattern to see if anything needs adjusting. Leave a strip of metal at the end of the cutter that is the same size as the beginning strip you left.

The cutter can be finished several ways. The easiest is to bend the cutter so that the beginning and the ending strip are flush with each other (as shown in the photo) and leave it at that. On the other hand, you can trim the end pieces, and bend them so that one is on the inside of the cutter and the other is on the outside. Then bond them with a good metal glue. Now you are ready to cut out clay shapes.

11 THE GREAT IMPOSTORS

Necklace of faux jade, turquoise, and rose quartz.

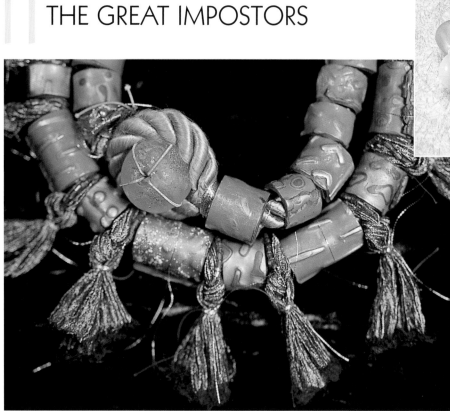

Namibian necklace by Louise Fischer Cozzi, a beautiful example of faux metal and stone.

It's impossible to explain here all of the techniques for transforming your clay into look-alikes of jade, ivory, bone, wood, amber, coral, jet, tortoiseshell, jasper, glass, etc. Polymer clay can be manipulated to look very much like these and many other substances. Look at the many books on beads through the ages, and the photos in this book, to see the possibilities. With a little experimentation, you will soon find a way to create just about any appearance you desire. Below are instructions for a few popular impostors to start you off.

Faux ivory, amber, cinnabar, and jade.

Jade

Translucent clay is a best friend of many of the impostors. Embossing powder is another. One very effective way to make faux jade is with a combination of translucent clay and several shades of green embossing powders. Embossing powders are worked into the clay, a small amount at a time. As a rule, the baked clay will be darker than it appears before baking when using this method, so be cautious with your additions of the powder.

Another nice jade effect uses translucent clay mixed with a small amount of green opaque clay and a tiny touch of orange to desaturate the green somewhat (make it grayer). A few tiny sprinkles of purple and/or black can add to the authentic appearance of the faux

jade. When adding any color to translucent clay, start with a very small amount of color and work up from there if necessary.

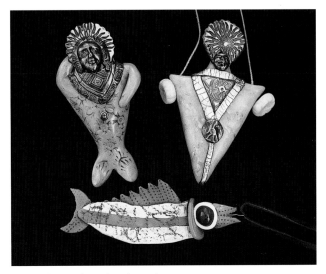

Faux jade pendants by the author.

Turquoise

Starting with a turquoise color of clay or a combination of turquoise and a small amount of green, depending on the type of turquoise you are trying to emulate, will give you nice results. The polymer clay should be chopped into tiny pieces or grains and then pressed together, but not so hard as to diminish the small individual bits of clay. You can also use a food processor to do the chopping. This will result in a rounder type of grain than if done by hand. If you will examine pieces of actual turquoise, you will easily see the result you want. Grate a small amount of black clay and add to the turquoise before forming your piece. Use a rough piece of tree bark to impress the surface of the clay to give further dimension to it. Antique the piece by rubbing burnt umber acrylic paint over it, making sure you hit all the recessed areas. Wipe the surface paint off with a paper towel. While the paint is still wet, press some dark potting soil or just plain earth into the clay, and brush off the excess. After baking, sand the surface, and then buff by machine or by hand.

A variety of faux turquoise by the author.

For a smoother type of turquoise, you can start with translucent clay and add turquoise-colored embossing powder and mix them together. Add a light sprinkling of black embossing powder and mix in slightly. Form your piece, bake, and then sand and buff.

Bone, Ivory, and Wood

Bone and ivory fauxs have been done many different ways by various clay artists. Sometimes just mixing an old ivory color of clay will be enough for your project. Some combinations for this are: white, beige/ecru and a bit of yellow; or try white and a small amount of gold; or beige/ecru and translucent. Play with the amounts until you find what works for what you have in mind. A more detailed method for doing ivory is to roll out long snakes of white, beige/ecru, and translucent and then bundle them together. Cut the bundles in three pieces and bundle again. Roll out the bundle into a long snake, cut in three pieces, bundle again, and roll out. Repeat this a number of times. As you do

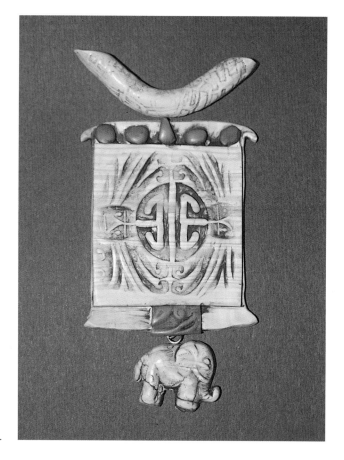

Faux ivory pin has "jade" parts added on.

this, the diameter of each of the original colors will become smaller. If you cut off an end piece from the snake, you can see just how small they are. If you go too far, however, the colors will blend together and you will lose the striated effect. When they are as small as you want them, cut them into three pieces, or six, depending on how wide you want the piece to be, and

Faux amber.

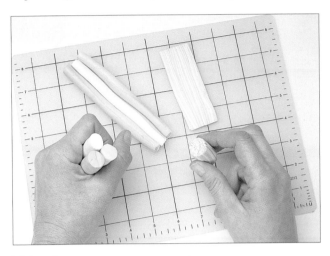

Making faux ivory.

place them side by side lengthwise, snuggling them close to each other. You can now roll them out lengthwise with a hand roller to the thickness you need for whatever project you are doing. If you roll sideways, your striations will get wider.

You can get the look of wood by varying this technique, using slightly darker tones, or wider striations.

Amber

Combining translucent clay with small amounts of opaque orange, a golden yellow, and a dark red such as bordeaux or alizarin crimson can make a beautiful amber look-alike. To do this, the translucent and yellow clays are mixed in a ratio of 1:1. Add only a very small amount of orange at a time, mixing well after each addition, until you get a nice warm tone. Add just a tiny bit of the red, as it is a highly saturated color. You will discover that you also can adjust the mixture to resemble a variety of coral tones. Some are very yellow, others are quite orange, and some have more red, for a darker effect.

Rose Quartz

Imitation rose quartz is easy to make. The mixture is made using translucent clay and a tiny bit of the alizarin crimson or bordeaux red. Add only the smallest amount of the red to begin with. You can always add more, but you can't take it out once it's in (although you can add more transparent to lighten the mixture). Mix the two together, but not all the way. You want to leave it marbled. Divide this mixture in half and set one half aside. Add a small amount more of the red clay to the remaining half and mix again to get a somewhat darker shade of pink. Roll both colors of pink out into small snakes. Chop both snakes into small thin pieces, or else grate them on a mini grater, letting the pieces mix together as you do. Your mix will now have light and dark areas. Now you can press the pieces of clay together and use it for whatever project you wish.

Faux rose quartz.

12 A POTPOURRI OF TECHNIQUES

Inclusions

You can mix a great many things into polymer clay for a wide variety of effects without damaging the structural integrity of the clay — for example, embossing powders, mica powders, mica flakes, colored and natural sand, fibers and threads, herbs and spices, and seeds. Jump in and experiment. Keep a record of what you do so that you can repeat your successes. Reminder: Be sure to wear a mask when working with powders.

Embossing Powders. Embossing powder mixed into polymer clay will give the baked translucent clay a convincing look of stone without the hard-to-deal-with fibers that are in stone-look clays. You can get many other effects besides stone. When embossing powder is added to layers of different colored clays, they take on many other appearances. There are no standard measurements for how much powder to use with a certain amount of clay. A lot of powder will cause the clay to be quite dark; a small amount will give a paler appearance.

Embossing powders can be purchased at almost all rubber stamp supply stores or from stamp suppliers on the Internet, as well as from polymer clay supply companies. With embossing powders, use translucent or tinted translucent clay only. Roll the clay into a sheet on the #1 setting (⅛", 3.2 mm) of the pasta machine; then spoon or shake about one-quarter of the amount of powder you plan to use onto one-half of the clay's surface. Leave a good margin of bare clay around the edges. Fold the unpowdered clay over on top of the powdered clay. Start by pressing in the middle of the piece and work toward the edges. This will help to eliminate most of the trapped air. Seal the edges of bare clay tightly. Run this "packet" of clay through the pasta machine on the #1 setting. You will still get a few air bubbles, but these will work out as you continue to mix. Fold the piece again and repeat running it through the machine. Continue doing this until the powder is evenly distributed throughout the clay. Repeat this with another quarter of the powder, and continue, until you have used it all. This process makes somewhat of a mess. Some powder may spill out, so put down paper towels or something else to catch it, then return it to the clay and keep mixing.

Mica Powders and Flakes. With mica powders and flakes, you can experiment with the amounts to see what results you get. These also require translucent clay for the best effects.

Kitchen and Garden Powders and Herbs. Colored or plain sand, seeds, herbs, and spices also need some experimenting. Starting with a level teaspoon of any one or more of these is a good beginning. Surprising results often occur when working with these inclusions. From the kitchen, try adding such things as black pepper, red cayenne pepper, pumpkin pie spice, rosemary leaves, oregano, dill seed, and coffee. From the garden, use a variety of flower petals such as rose, lavender, and gladiolas, as well as potting soil, sand, and bird seed. Dried flowers placed underneath a very thin layer of translucent clay make a lovely effect, rather like an impressionistic painting with diffuse colors.

Colored sand, embossing powder, and tiny beads are some inclusions you could use.

Fibers and Threads. Adding fibers and threads to tinted translucents can produce some striking results. Most all of these stand up well to the heat of the oven. Sandwiching them between two thin layers of the translucent clay is one way to use them. Another is to cut them into small segments and then mix them into the clay as you would the other inclusions.

Liquid Clay

Liquid Sculpey comes in opaque white and translucent. It can be tinted by adding mica powders or tiny amounts of oil paint (acrylic paint makes it bubble when baking because of the high water content). Tinted or untinted, Liquid Sculpey can be used to create various finishes on your clay. For instance, it can be dripped over the sides of a bowl or vase. It can be painted on and then rubbed off to simulate antiquing. A lovely verdigris patina can be made this way. To tint the liquid, pour into a glass dish the amount you think you will need for your project. Add mica powder, starting with a half-teaspoon (2.5 mL), or add oil paint by dipping a toothpick into the paint and then into the liquid clay. Stir the liquid until the color is completely mixed. If the shade isn't deep enough, add a bit more until you reach the shade you want.

Using a rubber stamp or mold to create "cells" in raw clay, which you then fill with colored liquid clay, you can create items that resemble cloisonne glass enamel work. Sanding and buffing will give the clay a glasslike shine.

Liquid Sculpey will not air-dry. Like all the other polymer clays, it must be baked.

Carving, Drilling, Sawing, and Cutting Clay

Clay that has been baked correctly can be easily carved, drilled, sawed, or cut. Woodworking tools or linoleum-cutting tools should be used if you wish to carve a pattern on a baked bead, vessel, pin, or other item. It's best to pencil in the lines for your carving

Baked clay is easily carved with a woodcarving tool.

first. On flat pieces, it's possible to do a black-and-white line drawing transfer when baking, and then use those lines for your carving.

Holes in beads for stringing cords can be made either before baking with a needle tool, knitting needle, or a wooden skewer, or they can be drilled after baking, using either a Dremel type tool, an electric drill with a very small bit, or a pin vise with a small bit.

Baked clay can be sawed with a jewelry saw or a small scroll saw or jig saw to just about any shape you wish. Thin sheets of baked clay can be cut with scissors. After doing any of these procedures, you may wish to sand the cut edges, as these methods often produce rough edges.

Eggshell Mosaics

This technique was developed by Jenny Dowde, who lives in Dapto, New South Wales. The eggshell mosaic can be used to make pins, pendants, earrings, bracelets, boxes, and anything else you might think of. The uses of these eggshells are endless.

The Basic Idea. You will need *some* washed eggshells for the mosaic. A wide variety of shapes and forms can be used for this fun technique. You may use a flat form, shape a cabochon, or encase the mosaic in a small frame. The mosaic can be set onto a piece of handmade paper so that the edges of the paper show around it. Tiny jewels can be glued on for such things as an animal's eyes, or just for a sparkle. Jones Tones foils or any of the iron-on types of foils that work on clay in the background add a lovely pearlescence to a piece.

For all of the pieces, cut out or form your shape in the background color of polymer clay you want. The clay should be rather soft. For Method 1, crush the eggshells into small pieces, approximately ⅛" to ¼" size (0.4 cm to 0.6 cm). For Method 2, leave them uncrushed to start.

Eggshell Method 1

1. Make a clay object the color and shape you want, but don't bake yet. Press the pieces of eggshell well into the clay wherever you want them to be, with the outside of the shell face up.
2. Antique the entire piece with any one of the following: oil paint or acrylic paint in just about any color, or

Center: Bits of dyed eggshell are pressed into clay, which may be cut with cookie cutters.

CREATIVE WAYS WITH POLYMER CLAY

Aleene's Enhancers in weathered iron or verdigris. A gold or copper wash of metallic acrylic paint that is diluted is beautiful.

3. Bake the piece. Sand the surface lightly with wet/dry sandpaper in 400 and 600 grits. Add more antiquing if you wish.

4. For a nice sheen you can coat with Future acrylic floor finish, thinned Translucent Liquid Sculpey, or a clay-compatible glaze, which protects the delicate shells.

Eggshell Method 2

1. Make a clay object the color and shape you want, but don't bake yet.

2. Paint or dye the eggshells with acrylic paints before crushing. Crush them, and then press them into the surface of your base clay, with the outsides of the shells either up or face down on the clay. You will get a different look with each of these methods. Shells that are placed with the inside up on the clay may break easily when sanding, however, and it is more difficult to adhere them to the clay. You may need to use some glue or a bit of Translucent Liquid Sculpey to adhere them. Skip the sanding.

3. Coat with Future floor finish, thinned Translucent Liquid Sculpey, or a clay-compatible glaze to protect the shells.

Here are some ideas you can use with either method:

1. Apply shells over Jones Tones background, antique with acrylic paint, and seal with Future floor finish.

2. Paint shells with blue acrylic paint before crushing. Apply shells to base, rub surface of shells with gold powder, bake, and seal with Future floor finish.

3. Stipple baked clay and shells with copper acrylic paint, let dry, sand lightly, and seal.

4. Apply shells to the surface of the clay and gently stretch the clay to open up the spaces between them. Antique before or after baking, or both.

5. Marble the shells with oil paints; let dry. Crush shells and apply to clay. Rub the piece with your choice of oil paint and let dry. Sand the piece to remove paint from the shells, but leave paint in the cracks. Rub the surface with Super Bronze Pearl-Ex; then seal.

6. After applying shells to the clay, make a mixture of Pearl-Ex silver and Future floor finish, and wash this over the piece. Wipe most of the silver off the surface of the shells, but leave it in the cracks. Bake.

Projects

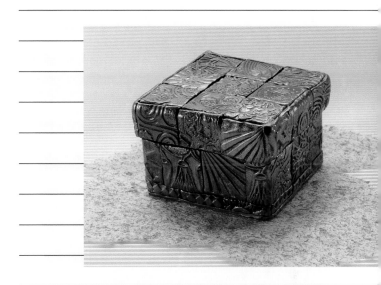

SCENIC LOAF PIN

Designer
Barbara Sosna

arbara is an art history buff from Austin, Texas, who developed this project in order to use up scrap clay. She has used an adaptation of several polymer clay techniques to make this pin, which resembles a mountain landscape. This same technique can be used to create earrings, pendants, and box tops.

MATERIALS

Polymer clay:

Waste clay or new clay in earth tones, browns, greens, blues, grays, and whites for sky, mountains, and ground, 8 to 10 oz (224 to 280 g)

Metallic gold and black for frame and decorations, or your preference, 2 oz (56 g)

Pasta machine

Sharp blade

Wet/dry sandpaper

Pin back

Glue

1. Visualize the landscape you wish to make. Make a rough sketch that shows the scene divided into foreground, mid-ground and background (or sky). Prepare sheets of clay about 3" by 6" (8 × 15 cm) in various thicknesses. Stack sheets of earth-tone clay for the foreground until the loaf is one-third the total size of what you want for the total loaf. The image will be formed by taking a slice from the side of the loaf.

2. To make a mountain, roll a log of clay and place it on top of the stacked earth-tone sheets, but run it from front to back of the stack, not along the width (see Photo 1). The end of the log is facing the front of the stack. Stack sheets, including some metallic colors, on top of the log and press them down on each side of the log. The log will cause the sheets on top of it to distort and will create organic forms for the mid-ground.

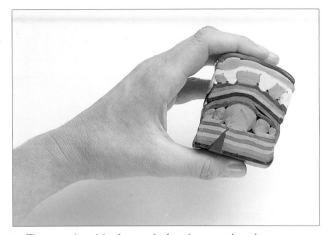

2. The completed loaf cane, before being reduced.

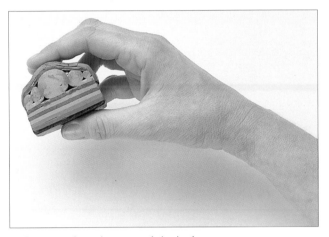

1. Begin stacking the parts of the loaf cane.

3. For the background or sky, add several sheets of lighter colors in tones of blue. Form the clouds by making logs of white and gray, and blends of these. Run these in the same direction as the log for the mountain. Cover the cloud logs with more sheets of various blues and continue until you feel the landscape is complete (Photo 2).

4. Important: Let the loaf rest at least overnight before reducing; then reduce it carefully by gently pressing and stretching it until it is the size and shape that you want. (See the Making Canes section of the book for reducing a cane.) Let it rest a little longer before slicing. Take thin slices off the side of the loaf with a sharp tissue blade or cane slicer such as the JASI™.

5. Roll out sheets of black and metallic gold clay (or other suitable colors) for the frame. Cut the gold to a size somewhat larger than your loaf slice. Cut the black slightly larger than the gold, and stack the two together with the gold on top for the backing (Photo 3). Lay your landscape slice on top of these two, and gently press together. Bake and let cool. Sand and buff to a soft sheen. Attach the pin back with glue and let dry.

This stacking loaf technique can be used for more than just landscapes. I'm sure you'll already be thinking of other effects that you can achieve with this method.

3. A cane slice is placed on a backing.

ROCK PURSE OR AMULET

Designer
Dotty McMillan

Some of the most incredible work done by any polymer clay artist is by Kathleen Dustin. Her work has adorned a number of polymer clay books, art books, magazines, and greeting cards. The term "rock purse" began with Kathleen when she began creating her stunning polymer purses, which are embellished with gracefully sculptured women along with an astonishing variety of colorful cane work. Kathleen's statement that she first began making these purses using an unusual-shaped rock as the mold set off a flurry of experiments by other clayers. Rock "amulets," miniature versions of a purse, have become the most popular.

An exciting element of making either the large or the small version of a rock purse is choosing a technique for its exterior. The choices seem endless. Why not let your imagination soar when designing yours? Some ways to go are: faux bone, ivory, jade, fake or hand-carved surfaces, mokume gane, cane work of all kinds, sculptured or molded elements, metallic surface, a stone-look appearance, and multi-media techniques. For this project, we will be making an impostor carved ivory amulet.

MATERIALS

Polymer clay:

  Waste clay, 6 to 8 oz (168 to 224 g)

  Gold Premo! Sculpey, 2 oz (56 g) or more,
  depending on the size of the rock you use

  White, about 3 oz (85 g)

  Beige/ecru (scraps)

  Translucent Liquid Sculpey (or Sobo glue)

Acrylic roller or pasta machine

Sharp blade or craft knife

Needle tool

Aluminum foil

Polyester stuffing: a handful

Mold release such as cornstarch or talc

Clay modeling tool

Burnt sienna acrylic paint and a stiff brush

Rubber stamps or molds in whatever patterns or designs you like

Wet/dry sandpaper in 320, 400, and 600 grits

Buffing equipment

Drilling equipment

Cyanoacrylate glue

Cord for hanging amulet (e.g., Buna-N flexible rubber cord)

1. Choosing a Rock. Choose a rock with a shape you like, or make a fake rock of your own (see Step 2). All you need for this is some aluminum foil and some waste clay. The rock size will determine the size and shape of your purse or amulet. When designing or choosing the shape of your rock, remember that down the line you will have to remove the rock from the inside of your purse or amulet. Decide where you will cut for the lid; then look to see if you will need to make more cuts in order to extract the rock. You can easily avoid extra cuts by modifying your design; or, if you are determined to do a design that will require them, don't despair, as the extra cuts can be concealed.

2. Making the Core for a Fake Rock. If you are using a real rock, skip this section and go on to Step 4. To begin your fake rock, take out a long sheet of aluminum foil and crumple it into roughly the shape you want for your finished purse. Compact it very tightly, even banging it down on a hard surface to accomplish this. Using more foil sheets, continue adding to the size of your shape, compacting as you go, until you reach the size that is slightly smaller than what you want your finished purse to be. Note: The layer of waste clay you will add later over the "rock" will make the rock somewhat larger, and the clay you use over that for your purse will also add to the size of the finished piece. If you are not careful, you will end up with an amulet that is quite a bit larger than you expected. Smooth, press, and bang the surface of the foil to make it as smooth and bumpless as possible.

3. Exterior of the Rock

a. Blend your waste clay into one solid color. Roll out a sheet of it on the #1 setting of the pasta machine (⅛" or 3.2 mm). The sheet must be large enough to cover the surface of your compacted foil shape (Photo 1). Form the clay around the shape, cutting and removing clay where necessary. When the foil shape is completely covered, carefully smooth the surface, using

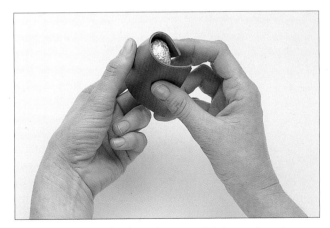

1. Wrap and smooth waste clay around foil to make a faux rock.

your fingers, rolling or pressing on a smooth surface, rolling in the palm of your hands, and any other way you find works well.

b. Lay your rock on a nest of polyester stuffing and place it in the oven. Bake for one hour at the temperature recommended by the clay manufacturer. You can bake even longer to insure a strong rock, as long as you watch that your temperature doesn't get too high. Remove and let cool. Wet-sand the polymer clay rock to make the surface nice and smooth.

4. Gold Clay Layer

a. Roll out a sheet of Premo! gold clay on the #4 setting (⁵⁄₆₄", 2 mm) of the pasta machine. Fold and roll it back through the machine until the mica particles on the surface are aligned and the clay is a shiny gold. Use one of the release agents on the surface of your rock. Begin covering the surface of the rock or fake rock with the gold clay (Photo 2). Stretch the gold clay slightly and curve the clay to fit the curve of the rock. Cut out areas of extra clay and continue until the entire piece is covered. If you have any overlapped areas where the clay is thicker than the rest, slice them down to size with a sharp blade and smooth them even with the rest of the surface.

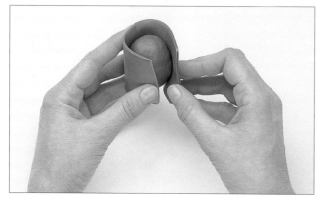

2. Wrap and smooth a baked faux rock or a real rock with gold clay.

b. Roll the rock against your work surface to smooth the clay. Roll in your hands, and also use your fingers to get the surface as nice and smooth as possible. This layer of gold clay will be the interior of your amulet.

5. Molded Outer Layer

a. To approximately 3 ounces (85 g) of white clay, add two pea-sized pieces of beige or ecru clay. Add a little more until you have a warm, creamy white. Roll out a sheet of the clay on the #1 setting (⅛", 3.2 mm) of the pasta machine. Coat your rubber stamp or mold with a release substance. Press the sheet of clay into or onto the stamp or mold (Photo 3). If the stamp or mold is smaller than the sheet of clay, move the clay and continue to impress the blank areas until the entire sheet has impressions on it.

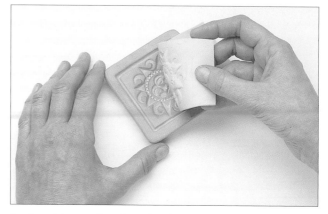

3. A mold is used to form the designs.

b. Carefully fit this sheet of clay around the amulet, covering the gold clay the same way you covered the rock or fake rock earlier. This is rather tricky as you don't want to wipe out the impressions you've made while doing this. Using a clay shaper or other clay modeling tool helps. You want to cut and fit and secure the clay. When the piece is covered, let it sit for an hour or so to firm up.

6. Cutting the Lid

a. At this point, cut the clay where you want the lid. A craft knife is best for doing this. It is easier if you score a line with your needle tool along where you want to cut, before you do the actual cutting. Check to see whether, after cutting, you will be able to take out the rock, or whether you will have to do extra cuts. When cutting, hold the craft knife at an angle so that the cut is beveled. This makes for a much neater fit between the lid and the bottom of the amulet.

b. After cutting, do not separate the lid from the bottom. Place the piece into the oven on a nest of polyester stuffing and bake at the temperature and for the length of time recommended by the clay manufacturer. Once your piece is baked, you may need to go around the cut again with your knife to loosen it. It may need a little coaxing to remove it from the rock. A very thin, small palette knife may help. Use it the way you would when helping a cake separate from the pan in which it was baked.

Note: Some people recommend that you wait to make the cut for the lid until the piece is baked and still quite hot. You then cut it, quickly remove the rock, fit the top and bottom back together, and then dip the whole thing into cold water. The clay will harden quite fast and, if you have positioned it well, the top will fit nicely. You may want to experiment with this cutting method also, to discover which is more successful for you.

7. Sanding. When your amulet is cool, wet-sand it, starting with the 320 grit sandpaper, to remove any slight irregularities. Sand lightly with this first grit, so you don't sand down the impressions. Then move on to the 400 grit, and then the 600. You can go higher if you like, but this will give you a nice finish. Complete this step by either hand-buffing the surface or using a buffing wheel.

8. Lip. To make certain the lid on your amulet doesn't slip and slide sideways while you are wearing it, you need to make a small clay lip around the edge of the bottom half of your piece (Photo 4). For this, roll out some of the gold clay on the #4 setting (⅝₄", 2 mm) of your pasta machine. Cut a strip that is ½"(1.2 cm) wide and long enough so that it fits completely around

the inside edge of the bottom half of the amulet. It should protrude above the edge of the piece by ¼" (0.6 cm). The other ¼" is the area that is attached to the inside of the amulet. To make sure it adheres to the already baked clay, either coat the inside edge of the baked clay with Translucent Liquid Sculpey before applying the lip piece, or coat it with Sobo glue and let it dry before applying. Either method will make sure the pieces will bond. Rebake the bottom piece for 20 minutes and let cool.

9. Antiquing. Using a rather stiff brush, antique the entire outside of the piece with burnt sienna acrylic paint. Use a jabbing motion all over the piece. This will insure that the paint goes into all the crevices. (See details in the Antiquing section of the book.) Wipe off the excess and let the paint dry. Give the piece another gentle buffing to bring back the shine.

10. Drilling Holes and Finishing

a. You will need a cord for your amulet so that you can wear it around your neck. Buna-N rubber cord is a good choice as it is smooth, stretchy, and comfortable to wear. You can use a hand drill, a Dremel tool, or a pin-vise fitted with a drill bit to drill two holes in the lid of the amulet where your cord will go through. Choose a drill bit that will accommodate the outside diameter of your cord. Mark the two places on the lid where you will drill. Carefully and slowly drill these two holes.

b. Take a cord, cut to the length you want it, and bevel each end with a sharp blade or knife. Fit one end into each of the two holes in the lid. Put some glue onto the beveled ends and attach the ends inside the bottom of the amulet. Let the glue set up for several hours. The lid will now be able to slide up and down on the cord and you won't lose it.

All you have to do now is to put some "mad money" into your little rock amulet, and you are ready to go on the town!

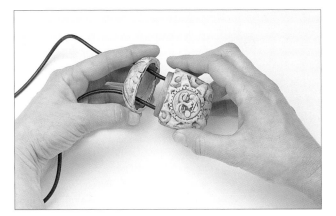

4. A lip of clay inside the bottom of the amulet keeps the lid in place.

FAUX CLOISONNE PENDANT

Designer
Carol Zilliacus

Many of Carol's polymer clay pieces have a lovely painterly appearance. Take a look at some of her other stunning pieces in the gallery section of the book. The great faux cloisonne technique shown here can be used for all sorts of items.

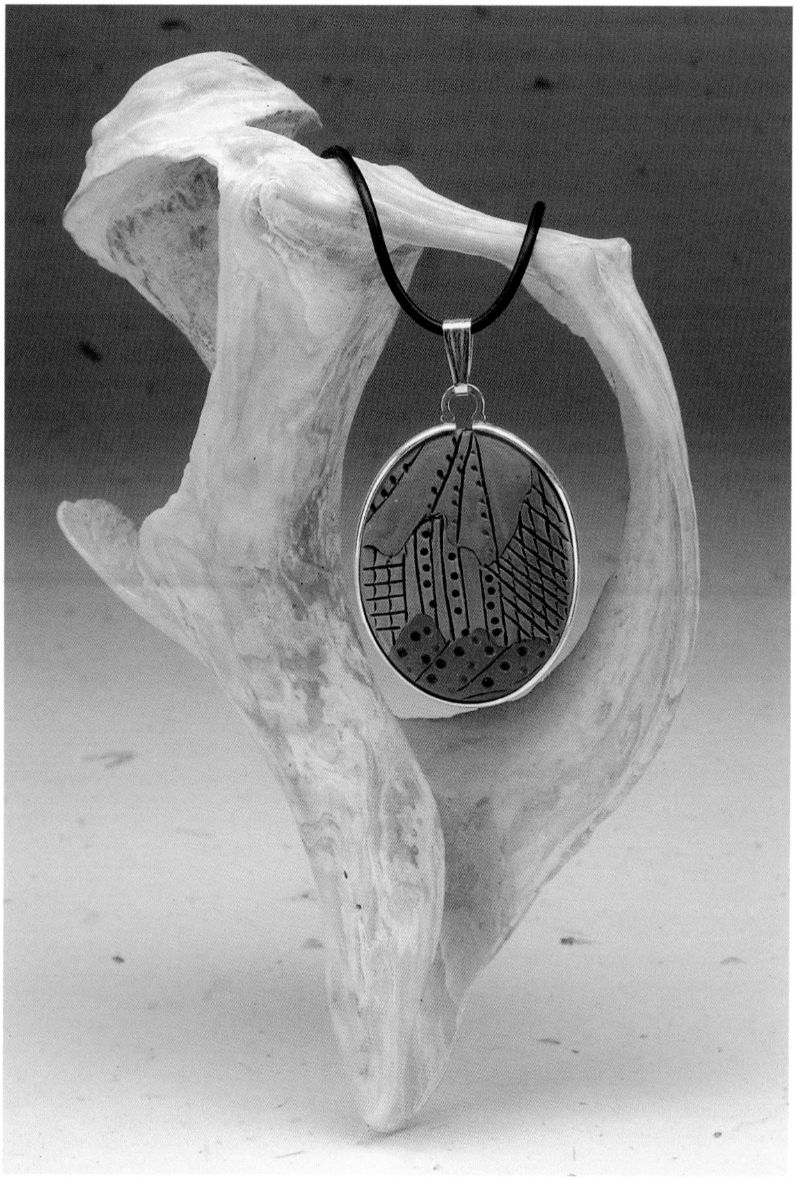

1. The Carol Zilliacus Variation of the Skinner Blend. The Skinner blend is a quick way of blending clay colors. It was described in the basic techniques section of the book. The following is a special variation that Carol Zilliacus developed for this project.

a. Condition the clay well. Roll out sheets of each color on the #1 setting (⅛", 3.2 mm) of the pasta machine. Cut each sheet of the three main colors (shown here: red, yellow, and blue) into tall triangles. Place them tip to bottom, slightly overlapping each other, in alternating colors. If you place complementary colors next to each other, you may get a muddy middle tone. On the other hand, this sometimes results in surprisingly beautiful results. Experiment.

b. Cut the sheet of white clay into small triangles, about one-third the length of the other triangles. Place these on top of all the other triangles (see Photo 1). Fold the sheet of triangles so that the bottom comes up to meet the top. Do not fold the clay from side to side. Run the folded sheet through the pasta machine,

MATERIALS

Polymer clay:

Three colors (shown here, red, yellow, and blue), 4 oz each (112 g)

White, 2 oz (56 g)

Gold Premo! Sculpey (metallic), 4 oz (112 g)

Pasta machine

Sharp blade

Aspic cutters: small shapes, e.g., a star, square, circle, rectangle, crescent moon, and oval

Bakery tissue or waxed paper

Plastic wrap

Burnishing tool*

Metal bezel and bale; silver works well

Buna-N cord, 1/16 or 1/8 size, or other decorative cord or chain for hanging a pendant

Clasp for cord

Needle tool or other sharp texturing tool

Small-diameter brass or copper tubes, for texturing clay

Cyanoacrylate glue

Exacto knife or other craft knife

Wet/dry sandpaper, from 600 to 1000 grit (found in auto supply shops)

Acrylic paint: burnt umber, or any color you prefer

Rags or towels

*Carol uses a wooden or ceramic knob from a cabinet door, 1" to 2" (2.5 to 5 cm) in diameter.

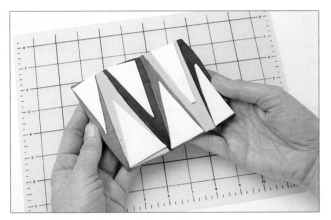

1. Carol Zilliacus's special Skinner blend.

folded end first, starting with the thickest pasta machine setting. Fold the sheet again, bringing the bottom up to the top, and run it through the pasta machine again. Repeat this 10 to 15 times, until the blend is smooth, but let some stronger bands of color still show. You will see magic! Your three primary colors are blending into all the colors of the color wheel, and they even have areas of very pale colors.

2. Cutting Your Shapes

a. Run the blended sheet through the pasta machine on the #3 setting (3/32", 2.4 mm). Run your sheet of conditioned gold clay through the pasta machine on the #3 setting. Place your blended sheet of clay on top of the gold sheet of clay and run them through the pasta machine together on the #3 setting.

b. Use your aspic cutters to cut out many shapes, making sure to leave a lot of space between them. Be sure you have a variety of colors in your cut pieces. Place the cut pieces on a sheet of bakery tissue or waxed paper.

c. Use a needle tool to pick up a shape and carefully reinsert the piece into your sheet, but into a different color area than the place from which it was cut (Photo 2). It is easy to insert the cut-out shape into an identical-shaped empty space. It is important to place the cut-out shapes into areas of your sheet where the greatest color contrast occurs. You might try reversing the cut-out shapes so the gold layer is on the top.

3. Burnishing and Cutting. Place bakery tissue or other transparent paper over the completed sheet of clay. Use the cabinet doorknob or other burnisher to

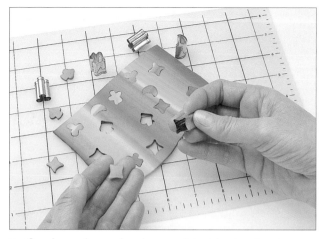

2. Cut shapes from colored areas of the blend and replace in different-colored areas.

4. Decorating Your Pendant. Examine your piece carefully. Try to mentally establish areas where you can either draw lines or texture in the clay. Look for places where there are shape or color changes. Practice drawing line designs on scrap clay. See what effect dragging your needle over the clay has. Using the needle tool like a pencil, draw straight and curvy lines. Now establish a pattern. Draw three straight lines in one direction and then in another. To achieve a textured look, carefully press the metal tubes into areas of your pendant. Practice on scrap clay first. You need to find out how hard to press without tearing the clay. Experiment using other tools for decorating your pendant. When you know what you want to do, make your patterns and textures on the actual pendant. When you have finished decorating your pendant, set it aside.

5. Beads and Baking. Make two round beads from black clay, with holes large enough so two strands of cord can fit through. They will be used to hold the clasp in place. This is not necessary if you use a chain. Place the pendant, which is still in the bezel, and the beads on a sheet of bakery tissue and bake at the manufacturer's recommended temperature for 30 minutes. Fill a container with cold water. Keep it near the oven. Immediately after baking, lift the bakery tissue with

smooth and polish the surface. Remove the tissue and replace it with plastic wrap to protect the clay from unnecessary marks. Carefully and lightly slide the oval or round bezel over your sheet until you find an area you like. Press the bezel gently so you can see its outline. Remove the plastic wrap and press the bezel into the clay (Photo 3). Use a craft or Exacto knife to cut the pendant shape so that it fits into the bezel. Gently insert the clay into the bezel, and set both onto a bakery tissue or waxed paper.

3. Use the bezel to choose and cut out the shape for the pendant.

FAUX CLOISONNE PENDANT

the pendant and beads still on it and dunk it into the water in the container. The cold water will intensify the colors in your work.

6. Sanding. When your pendant is cool, pop it out of the bezel. Be sure to note how the pendant is placed in the bezel. Wet your pendant and the 600-grit sandpaper and gently sand your work. Rinse the pendant when you change the sandpaper to a higher grit. The trick to sanding is not to press heavily on your work.

7. Embossing and Buffing. Choose a contrasting color of acrylic paint to emboss your work. Burnt umber is a good choice. Cover your work with the paint. Carefully wipe the paint from the surface with a soft rag or paper towels. You may need to either wet the pendant or your rag to remove extra paint. Paint will still adhere in the grooves and lined areas. All the areas you decorated will stand out now. Buff the piece, making sure that all of the paint is completely dry.

8. Gluing the Pendant to the Bezel. Put a drop of glue on a piece of paper. Use a toothpick or anything with a sharp point. Dip the point into the glue. You only need a tiny drop. Now transfer the glue from the toothpick to the inside of the bezel. You need to drop a small amount of glue on both sides, at the top, and on the bottom. Carefully place your pendant into the bezel. Do this with the decorated side facing you. Try to get it set right the first time. The glue does not like to be disturbed. Immediately wick off any extra glue, using a paper towel.

9. Finishing. Thread the cord through the bale. Loop the cord through the clasp and glue it to itself with a drop of glue just below the clasp. Do the same at the other end of the cord for the jump ring. Your faux cloisonne pendant is now finished and ready to wear.

5. Three faux cloisonne pendants by Carol Zilliacus.

ANTIQUE CRACKLE-TILED TRAY

Designer
Barbara A. McGuire

arbara is a creative and talented artist who has written a much-needed polymer clay book, *The Foundations in Polymer Clay Design*. She has also designed special clay stamps that can be used two ways. One side is a regular stamp, while the other side is a mold of the stamp. Barbara's beautiful clay work has been a great inspiration to many polymer clay artists.

Barbara's beautiful tray appears to be made of old, crackled tiles. Once you have made this ancient-looking tray, your friends will have a tough time figuring out how you did it. Why not also try these same techniques for making unique jewelry, for decorating boxes, and for myriad other things I'm sure you'll come up with?

MATERIALS

Polymer clay:

    White #0 FIMO Soft, 2 oz (56 g)

    Black FIMO Soft, 2 oz (56 g)

    Brown FIMO Soft, 2 oz (56 g)

Thin sharp blade or knife

Quilting grid or graph paper

Card paper stock for baking

4 rubber picture stamps*

Cornstarch and brush

Burnt sienna acrylic paint and oil paint, and brush

Wet/dry sandpaper, 400 grit

Crackle finish such as Crafter's Pick Craqueleur™ base coat and top coat finishes

Burnt sienna oil paint (as recommended on crackle finish)**

Varnish (as recommended on crackle finish)**

Crafter's Pick® Ultimate Tacky glue or strong white glue

*Creative Claystamps Asian series is shown, but you can make your own stamps. See the section of the book on rubber stamps and molds.
**Different crackle finishes require different procedures, varnishes, and paints. Always test your product for compatibility.

1. Making the Checkered Tiles. Roll a thin slab of white clay on setting #4 (⁵⁄₆₄ inch or 2 mm) on the pasta machine. Align the slab over a measuring grid or graph paper, and cut a 4-inch square of clay, using a sharp, straight blade. Cut the square into 1" (2.5 cm) strips and then cut them crosswise into 1" squares. Pull out every other square, as in a checkerboard, and coat each one pulled out lightly with cornstarch. This acts as a release powder for the stamp. Stamp a partial image into each of the pulled-out squares. It is fine if the design runs off the edge or only a portion of the design shows. Another way to do this is to stamp the clay first and then cut eight 1" square pieces from the stamped clay and cut eight 1" square unstamped pieces (Photo 1).

2. Baking. Straighten or trim any edges that may have gotten distorted. If you don't like the design in any of the squares, simply recut and stamp another 1" square.

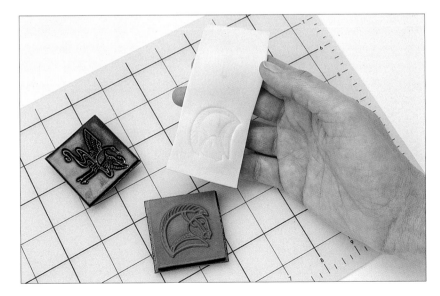

1. White clay is impressed with stamps and then is cut into equal-sized squares.

Reassemble, pressing the squares together. Bake all the squares in a block, face down on card stock paper. The squares should stay together.

3. Paint, Sand, Crackle

a. When the block is cool, paint the front of the squares with burnt sienna acrylic paint. Let the paint dry and then wet-sand the block. The paint will be removed except in the stamped images and the lines dividing the sections.

b. Apply the crackle base coat. Allow the piece to dry completely. The surface will be sticky to accept the top coat. Apply the crackle finish top coat. Allow the top coat to dry for at least 8 hours. Apply a thin layer of oil paint (burnt sienna) with a soft rag. It should flow into the cracks. Coat with a varnish recommended on the crackle finish.

4. Making the Tray

a. Combine and condition the black and brown clay together. Roll a slab ⅛" (3.2 mm) thick (#1 setting on the pasta machine), and place the checkered piece in the center of the slab. Trim the slab to extend ½" (1 cm) from the checkered piece. Remove the checkered piece and place the slab face-down on a sheet of card stock for baking.

b. Using the trimmed edges of clay, roll the black/brown clay into a cylinder and slice it in half lengthwise, creating two long half-cylinders. Place these two pieces on the bottom of the slab, making two "feet" or runners (Photo 2). Bake the entire piece.

5. Gluing. When the slab is finished baking, coat all

2. A log, cut in half lengthwise, forms the footing for the tray.

the backs of the checkered pieces with Crafter's Pick Ultimate Tacky glue or other strong white glue, and attach them to the slab while the latter is still hot.

Note: The pieces were glued in the last step to avoid putting any of the crackle finishes in the oven.

PUFF BEADS

Designer
Dotty McMillan

hese beads are not only fun to make, but also very comfortable to wear as pendants or centerpiece beads, as they can be made really large and still be lightweight because they are hollow. They are reversible, so you can switch them from one side to the other whenever the mood, or your outfit, requires it. One side is textured with a pattern and the other side is adorned with a photo transfer in this project. You could make both sides in the same color tones, or they could be totally different. The combinations are endless. The puff bead in this project is large, approximately 2" (5 cm) in diameter; it makes for a lovely centerpiece or pendant bead. The same technique can also be used to make larger or smaller beads.

1. Forming the Bead Mold

a. You need to make a mold of half the bead, but in order to make the mold for the puff beads, you must first make a bicone template of waste clay, bake it, and then press the baked bicone into a pad of waste clay in order to form the necessary concave mold to shape one-half of your bead. To form the bicone template, roll a smooth ball of waste clay that is the diameter you want for your finished bead (in our example it's 2", or 5 cm, wide). Use the jar lid to turn the ball into a bicone (oval, tapering to a cone at each end), as follows. Hold the lid from the top with your thumb and all four fingers. Photo 1 shows hand position for rolling a bead. Press down slightly and begin rolling in one direction. Straighten the bead with fingers, if necessary. Gently flatten the points of the bicone by press-

MATERIALS

Polymer clay:

    Gold Premo! Sculpey, 1 oz (28 g) per bead*

    White Premo! Sculpey, 1 oz (28 g) per bead

    Waste clay (mud) well mixed, 4 oz (112 g)

    Translucent Liquid Sculpey (optional)

Jar lid from wide-mouth jar

A copy-shop copy, laser print, or pencil drawing of a graphic for one side of the bead

Circle cutter set or 2¼" (5.7 cm) diameter circle cutter

Acrylic paint: metallic bronze and burnt sienna

Small flower shape cutter

Needle tool or small drill

Sharp blade

Cornstarch or talcum powder

Pasta machine or roller

Molds or stamps for texturing

Cyanoacrylate glue (Zap-a-Gap, Hot Stuff, PicStic, or similar)

Wet/dry sandpaper in 320, 400, and 600 grits

14K gold-fill wire (6", 15 cm) or any other type of sturdy craft wire

Buffing equipment

Colored pencils (optional)

*Regular Sculpey isn't strong enough.
**You can make a flower cutter if you don't have one. See the Creating Your Own Cutters section of the book.

1. Starting to roll a bicone bead using a jar lid.

ing downward on them with the jar lid. At the same time you are pressing gently downward, roll the ball around slightly to insure that the points will be somewhat rounded. Don't flatten the points too much, as you want as deep a dome as possible on each side (Photo 2, left). If you are unsure of how to make an evenly shaped bicone this way, shape this piece by hand. Bake the bicone template and let it cool. Sand the surface a little to insure that it is nice and smooth. **b.** Using waste clay, make a pad that is about ¼" (0.6 cm) deeper than one-half of the bicone template. Slowly, with a firm pressure, press the baked bicone template into the pad of waste clay until one-half of it is embedded in the pad. Don't go beyond the outer circular ridge of the bicone. You only need a mold that is the shape of one-half of your finished bead, because for each bead you will make two halves and put them together. Remove the bicone template and bake the mold for one hour at the recommended temperature for your brand of clay. Let the mold cool. Then dust it with cornstarch or talcum powder.

2. Making the Puff Bead

a. Roll out a sheet of gold clay on the #3 setting (3⁄32", 2.4 mm) of the pasta machine. Cut out a 3" (7.5 cm) square from the sheet. Impress the surface of the clay square with a rubber stamp, a mold from a rubber stamp, or a plastic texture sheet (used for scratch art). **b.** Using the circle cutter, cut out a 2¼" (5.7 cm) diameter circle from the clay, centering it on the impressed pattern. With the impressed pattern facing the bead mold, place the cut-out circle on top of the puff bead mold (Photo 2, right) and gently and slowly press it into the mold. Make sure the piece is centered in the mold. Press the center portion first, but don't press too hard, as that will stretch the clay. Urge the clay around the edges to slide down into the mold. Once the piece is pretty much down into the mold, take the baked bicone shape you made earlier and gently set it into and on top of the piece in the mold (Photo 3). Press it down as far as it will go. This is the same piece you used to make the mold, so it will fit nicely back into the mold. This bicone shape will insure that the clay will stay down and conform well with the mold. Leaving the bicone in place, bake and cool the piece and remove it from the mold. Set it aside.

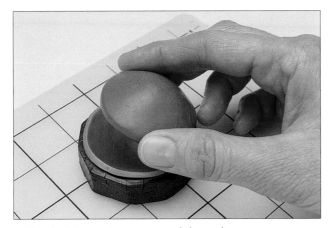

2. Left: Bicone bead and cutter. Right: Cut out a circle of gold clay and place it in the mold.

3. Set the bicone piece on top of the circle.

Faces for photo transfer side of bead.

3. Transfer Side of Bead

a. Roll out a 3" (7.5 cm) sheet of white clay and cut out a 2¼" (5.7 cm) circle with the cutter. Cut out your graphic so that it fits inside the circle. (See the Image Transfers section of the book for preparation of a graphic.) Color your graphic with colored pencils if you wish. Lay the graphic face down against the surface of the circle of unbaked white clay and burnish it well. Leave this piece sitting for at least an hour. The longer you leave it, the better your transfer. Don't move or touch the transfer during this time.

b. Gently and very slowly lift the transfer paper off the circle. Let the piece sit for another hour. This helps the toner to set up somewhat and helps avoid smearing. Repowder the mold and very gently place the circle of clay with the design face down onto the mold. Using your finger, begin to press the clay circle into the mold, urging the sides to also move into the mold. Set the bicone template into and on top of the clay and press down slowly and gently as you did for your first bead half. Be sure to keep your fingers away from the toner.

c. Bake the circle and mold for the recommended time for the clay you use. Let cool. Remove from mold and rub the outer surface of the piece with a soft cotton towel to smooth off any powder or bits of loose clay.

4. Assembling the Bead. Now it is time to put the two halves of the bead together. Run a small line of glue around the edge of one-half. There is a very thin edge on both these bead halves, so be careful not to use more than a tiny bit of glue. Fit the two halves together and hold for about 30 seconds. Let the glue cure for about 15 minutes.

5. Making the Flowers

a. While the glue is setting up, roll out a sheet of gold clay on the #3 setting (3/32", 2.4 mm) of the pasta machine. Cut out approximately 20 tiny flower shapes with the flower cutter. Make a small dot impression in the center of each flower. Using your needle tool, make three lengthwise lines on each of the petals (Photo 4).

5. Add flowers around both sides of the bead.

4. Use a tiny cutter to cut out flowers. Mark the petals with a needle tool.

b. On one side of the bead, place a circle of flowers side by side around the outside edge (Photo 5). Place a tiny drop of glue on one of the petal edges before pressing it against the baked clay edge. Turn the piece over and place the rest of the flowers around that side, matching them to the ones on the other side. Bake on polyester stuffing and let cool.

6. Sanding and Buffing.
Sand only the gold clay surfaces of the piece using the wet/dry sandpaper, starting with the 320 grit, then the 400 grit, and finishing with the 600 grit. This is not an easy piece to sand, so take your time and do it carefully. Don't press too hard with your sandpaper as you do not want to remove the impressions. *Do not sand the surface of the clay with the transfer as this would remove the transfer.* Buff the entire piece (being very gentle with the transfer surface) on a buffing wheel, or use a soft piece of cotton material.

7. Antiquing.
The bead is now ready to antique. For the gold surfaces, use the metallic bronze paint, dabbing it on with a stiff brush to make certain it goes into all the crevices. Rub the paint with your fingers to insure it has reached every area. Wipe the excess paint off until you are happy with the results.

Apply a small amount of the burnt sienna acrylic paint to the white transfer surface and wipe off the excess. This will give it a warm glow. Some of the bronze paint may find its way onto the white surface, which won't matter at all. Just wipe and work with the piece until it looks the way you want it to.

8. Hanging the Bead.
Make a small hole at the top of the bead using a needle tool or small drill. Run the piece of gold wire through the hole and form a loop. Secure the loop with several twists of the wire around it. Slip a gold chain through the loop and your beautiful puff bead is ready to wear.

Now that you understand the basics of making a puff bead and also how to get an image to transfer to a rounded surface, try your hand at variations. Make small puff beads and link them together for a necklace. Make a pair of matching earrings. You do not have to use the elaborate flowered edge that is on the bead you just made; make a very simple one using a thin snake of clay around the edge. Texture the snake, gild it, or leave it plain. Make a puff bead with mokume gane on both sides. Make one with a rainbow of cane slices (see the Making Canes section of the book). The variety possible is endless.

MAGIC NATASHA BEAD NECKLACE*

Designer
Dotty McMillan

These beads by any other name would be just as easy and fun to make. Many of will no doubt already know how to do this. Therefore, this is mainly for the newbies, or for those more experienced clayers who have not yet been exposed to it. Natasha Flechsig introduced this technique to the polymer clay world, where it fast became a favorite way to use up leftover bits of clay and canes. Hint: If your canes or clay bits have bright colors and lots of contrast, they will make your magic beads really sing!

*These are sometimes called mirror-image beads or Rorschach beads.

MATERIALS

Polymer clay:

    Lengths of canes you don't like or are tired of, distorted ends of canes, bad slices, and anything else with a pattern in it, about 6 oz (336 g) for the necklace shown

    Black clay, 1 oz (28 g)

Roller

Sharp blade

Needle tool

Spacer beads or other small beads

Necklace cord and catch

1. Making the Loaves. Combine a variety of your cane slices. For each bead you will need enough to make a log that is about 1" long (2.5 cm) and ½" (1 cm) wide. Roll the canes together into a ball, and then into a small log. Twist the log a turn or two to distort the patterns in the clay. Shape the log into a rectangular loaf, using the roller to square off the edges and smooth the sides (Photo 1).

2. Slicing and Assembling

a. Using a sharp blade, slice each rectangular loaf in half lengthwise and then open it up as if you were opening a book, keeping both halves together. You will immediately see that each half has a pattern that is symmetrical with the pattern on the other half (Photo 2).

1. Left to right: Bits and pieces of canes are rolled together, twisted, then formed into a loaf shape.

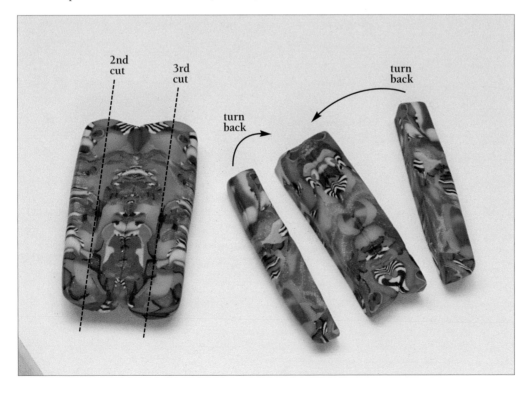

2. The loaf is cut in half and opened out (left); then the halves are cut in half. At right, two center quarters were reassembled, and two outer quarters will be turned to the back to make the back half of the Natasha bead.

b. Cut each of the halves in half again. When you roll each of the cut outer quarters back, you will see that they too have symmetrical patterns. You have actually turned the rectangular solid inside out. Push the four quarters together and smooth to make a bead. If you have done this correctly, all four sides have symmetrical patterns (Photo 3). If desired, add end pieces of black clay to some of the beads (see Photo 4).

3. Finishing. Use a needle tool to make a hole lengthwise through the length of each of the beads; then bake. Make as many beads as you want for a necklace. These long beads are lovely when sanded and buffed.

4. Center Pendant. If you wish to make a Natasha bead pendant, as shown on the necklace, stop with the first cut. After opening the bead following the first cut, gently roll over the surface with a roller to smooth it out. Trim the sides all around. Make a rectangle of black clay about 3" × 1½" (7.5 cm × 4 cm), and roll up the ends like a scroll, leaving room for the necklace cord to pass through the roll at one end. Press the sliced Natasha bead onto the black clay to attach. Bake, sand, and buff.

Variation: Instead of leaving the beads as rectangular solids, you can roll into rounded shapes. Or try cutting the rectangular solids in half and gently pinching the ends so that they take on the appearance of seed pods. There are many other ways to manipulate a magic bead, which you will no doubt discover if you experiment with them.

3. The quarters all assembled form beads with mirror images on all sides.

4. Some finished beads.

FAUX ETCHED GLASS BEADS

Designer
Dotty McMillan

Shhhh, don't tell anyone they aren't real. I have always admired necklaces with glass beads that have been etched with acid to give the surface a matte finish. I like the subtlety of them. They don't shout. You can somewhat see into them, and what you see looks deep and mysterious. However, an entire necklace of large glass beads can be extremely heavy to wear. The solution to this is to make faux etched-glass polymer clay beads, which look remarkably like the real thing, but weigh much less. These beads are extremely easy to make.

MATERIALS

Polymer clay:

Translucent Premo! Sculpey, 4 to 6 oz (112 to 168 g)

Tiny bits of bright red, orange, fuchsia, gold, and copper clay, any brand, for tinting

Black or dark color of clay, 1 oz (28 g)

Texturing items such as a knitting needle, Phillips screwdriver, wavy blade, star-shaped plastic furniture leg protector, and any other object that will make a distinct impression on the clay. These are used in making your mokume gane pad

Needle tool

New, very sharp blade

Paper towel

Sheet of waxed paper

Thread or fishline for stringing beads

Spacer beads (optional)

Necklace fastener

Mokume gane pad slices will be attached to the base bead.

1. Mokume Gane Slices. See instructions in the Impressed from the Top Mokume section of the book for details of how to do Step 1. Form a mokume gane "pad" using tinted translucent sheets. Tint each sheet with one of the colors listed above. Add a dark layer of clay on the top and impress the pad with interesting designs. The pad should be approximately 1" (2.5 cm) thick. The width and length aren't important. Just be sure you have enough to make the amount of beads you desire. Anchor your pad to your work surface so that it doesn't move when pushed or pulled. Using your new, sharp blade, take fairly thin slices and set the slices aside on a piece of waxed paper (photo). When the paper is filled with slices, begin making base beads.

2. The Beads. Roll out base beads using translucent clay a little smaller than you want your finished bead to be. Place mokume slices on the surface of the base bead and press firmly. Roll the bead first on your work surface, then between your hands, until it is round and smooth. Make a hole through the bead using the needle tool. Set the beads onto polyester stuffing on your baking surface and bake them at the regular temperature for 20 minutes; then turn the oven to 300°F (149°C) for 5 minutes, overbaking to darken them. When they are done, plunge them into a bowl of ice water and let them sit for 5 to 10 minutes. While your beads are chilling, why not take the time to make some small matching beads for earrings? Make spacer beads also, if you wish.

3. Finishing. When your beads are cool, string them together, adding spacer beads, and add a fastener. A sterling silver fastener looks beautiful with these faux glass beads.

Of course, you can make these beads in a variety of other colors. Take a look at some real glass beads for ideas. A wonderful book on glass beads, *Making Glass Beads* by Cindy Jenkins, is a great inspiration for polymer clay artists, as many of the beads in the book can be reproduced using polymer clay.

CHINA SHARD PINS

Designer
Dotty McMillan

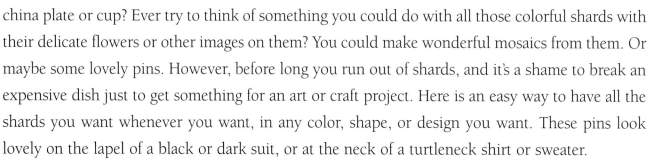

Have you ever had the misfortune to break a lovely china plate or cup? Ever try to think of something you could do with all those colorful shards with their delicate flowers or other images on them? You could make wonderful mosaics from them. Or maybe some lovely pins. However, before long you run out of shards, and it's a shame to break an expensive dish just to get something for an art or craft project. Here is an easy way to have all the shards you want whenever you want, in any color, shape, or design you want. These pins look lovely on the lapel of a black or dark suit, or at the neck of a turtleneck shirt or sweater.

MATERIALS

Polymer clay:

> White, 2 oz (56 g) or more
> Simple flower canes in whatever colors you like*
> Small amount of waste clay, 1 oz (28 g) or less

Krylon 18K gold leafing pen

*See Making Canes section of book for cane instructions.

Sharp blade

Brayer or acrylic roller

Pasta machine

Talcum powder

Wet/dry sandpaper in 320, 400, 600, and 1500 grits

Buffing wheel, Dremel tool, or a soft cotton towel

Pin backs

1. Roll out a sheet of white clay on the #3 setting (³⁄₃₂", 2.4 mm) of the pasta machine, and cut it into a rectangle. The size of the rectangle isn't important but, since you will be covering it with cane slices, be sure it isn't too large for your supply of canes. Place the white clay on a sheet of waxed paper. Take as many fairly thin slices from the flower canes as needed to cover the sheet of white. When it is completely covered, place another sheet of waxed paper on top. Using your roller or brayer, begin to roll and smooth the canes until the whole surface is all one level (Photo 1). If the paper begins to wrinkle and mar the clay surface, remove it and replace it with a smooth piece of paper. When the entire sheet is completely smooth, remove the paper and run it back through the pasta machine on the #2 setting (⁷⁄₆₄", 2.8 mm).

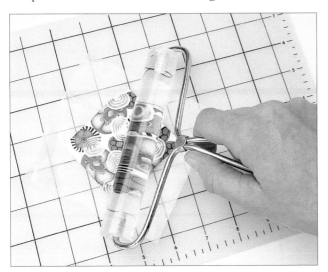

1. Cane slices are rolled smooth between sheets of waxed paper.

2. Tap out a small amount of talcum powder onto the surface of the clay sheet and spread evenly around. Using your fingertip, begin to polish the surface of the clay. Don't push too hard, as you don't want to smear the patterns. The talc acts as a smoothing substance.

3. Look over the patterns on the clay and decide which areas you like best. Cut out irregularly shaped pieces, as you might see with shards of china. You can probably cut out a number of shards from this one sheet of clay. Set these shards aside for now.

4. Using some of the waste clay, form several snakes or mounds of clay about ¼" (0.6 cm) thick, and then flatten them slightly. They should be slightly wider than the widest of your cut-out shards. These are the molds you will use to shape your shards. Shards are seldom flat all over. Bake these molds and let cool.

5. When your molds are cool, coat the back sides of your cut-out shards with talc, and then place one shard over each one of the molds, so that part of the shard is bent slightly (Photo 2). Bake. Plunge the shards into cold water while still very hot.

2. A cut-out shard shape is laid over a small prebaked mold.

6. Sand both sides of the baked shard, as well as the edges. Buff the edges and top (pattern side) only. Using a Krylon gold pen, go around the buffed edges. Let a little bit of the gold edge show from the top of the piece.

7. Glue your pin back to the piece with cyanoacrylate glue, let dry, and it's ready to wear.

EASY BREEZY BRACELET

Designer
Dotty McMillan

Bangle bracelets are not only fun to make, but also fun to wear. This one can be created to match any mood you happen to be in, or any outfit you want to wear. You can make this one fit snugly against your wrist or hang loose. It can be decorated with cane slices, mokume gane, faux ivory or jade, faux carving, mica powders, and just about anything else you can think of.

MATERIALS

Polymer clay:

    Base clay of your choice or waste clay, 2 oz (56 g)*

    Cane slices or other additions, such as are listed above**

    Small amount of clay for small rings

Wooden skewer, knitting needle, or metal rod

Elastic cord

Glue

Sharp blade

Measuring tape

*Decide how you want your finished bracelet to look. If it's the jade, ivory, or another faux look, that will be your base clay; see the Great Impostors section of the book for recipes for those base clays. If you are doing a bracelet totally covered with canes or mokume slides, you can use waste clay for the base; if the base color will show, choose a color you like.
**See the Techniques section of the book for how to make cane slices, mokume gane, etc.

1. Starting Out. Measure your wrist to determine what size your bracelet should be. Condition and mix the color of clay you've decided on for your base clay and then roll a ball 2½" (6 cm) in diameter. Roll the ball into a log 11½" (4 cm) long. With a blade, make a slice lengthwise on the log; but only go through to the center of the log, and open up the clay a bit to place the skewer into the cut opening in the clay (Photo 1). Snug the clay back into a log around the skewer. Leave the skewer in place. The elastic holding the two halves of the bracelet will fit here.

1. Center the skewer inside the cut log of clay.

2. Rolling the Length. Note: If you are doing a faux style bracelet, you are ready to roll out the length of bracelet. If you are using cane or mokume slices, you may want to add your slices now, before the length of the bracelet is rolled. This will result in the canes being elongated. If you wait until the bracelet is partially rolled out before adding slices, the canes will be less elongated. On the other hand, you can add canes or other decorations after the piece has been rolled to the correct length. It all depends on the look you want. Begin to roll the clay with the palms and heels of your hands, pulling outward as you do, stretching the clay somewhat. Don't try to do this fast. The clay will have a tendency to stick to the skewer, so stop and give it a turn to free it now and then. When the piece is 8" to 9" (20 to 22 cm) long, gently remove it from the skewer. Make small clay rings, if desired, by rolling a few thin logs of clay, twisting them, and shaping into circles about 1¼" (3 cm) in diameter.

3. Shaping and Baking. Place the clay bracelet on your baking surface and form it into an oval. Trim it to the correct size to fit. Cut the ends so that they are neat and smooth and fit right next to each other. The ends should be slightly off center to the curve of the oval. Bake and let cool. Bake the small rings.

4. Cutting and Stringing. With a very sharp blade, cut the baked oval on the opposite side from where the two cut ends meet (Photo 2). You will now have two identical halves of your oval. String the elastic through both pieces, add the small rings, secure the elastic with a knot, and trim the elastic ends. Poke the knot into one of the holes so that it does not show, and secure with glue.

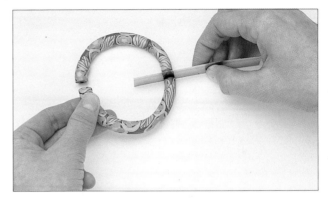

2. Cut the baked bracelet in half.

Alternative: While stringing, you may add purchased or handmade filler beads at the free ends. This is also a good way to enlarge a bracelet. Other items can be added to your bracelet before stringing. Snakes made around a wooden dowel that has a slightly larger diameter than your bracelet look handsome twisting around the bracelet. Just be certain that you make the bracelet larger than you normally would, as the additions reduce the open area that your wrist fits into. To wear the bracelet, pull apart and slip it over your wrist.

3. After baking, thread elastic through both halves and add clay rings, if desired.

HAPPY FACE PAPERWEIGHT

Designer
Dotty McMillan

*M*any people love to collect paperweights. This is the perfect gift for your collecting friends; you can be certain they won't have another one like it. Or maybe you could start your own collection. The designs for paperweights are endless. The main thing to remember is that they need to be heavy, so don't be tempted to make the inside with aluminum foil or leave it hollow.

1. Making the Base. Mix the waste clay well and form into a round column that is approximately 2" in diameter × 2½" high (5 cm × 6.5 cm); set aside. This is the core or base of the paperweight.

2. Making a Frame for the Jewel on the Lid. You need to make one-half of a small puff bead. The puff bead's outer diameter should be about 2½" (6.5 cm). The jewel will fit into the 1" (2.5 cm) hole cut in the center of the half puff bead. Refer to the project on making Puff Beads, page 62. Be sure to texture your sheet of clay before cutting out the circle for the puff bead half. Use a stamp or mold that gives a nice, deep texture. Lightly gild the raised texture areas with copper mica powder. Cut out a circle, using a 2¾" (7 cm) diameter circle cutter. Before putting the clay circle into the puff bead mold, cut a 1" (2.5 cm) circle out of the center (Photo 1). Place the circle that has the cutout center in the mold, bake, and cool. Coat the top of this piece with glaze to protect the copper powder, and let dry. You have now made a frame for a jewel.

MATERIALS

Polymer clay:

    Black, 1 oz (28 g)

    Copper, 3 oz (84 g)

    Translucent, ½ oz (14 g)

    Ultramarine blue, small amount

    Waste clay: about a pound (450 g)

    Translucent Liquid Sculpey

Puff bead mold, 2½" diameter (6.3 cm)*

Circle cutter, 2¾" (7 cm) diameter

Mica or metallic powder: copper

Texture mold or stamp

See Puff Bead project for bead mold information.

Set of circle cutters

Armorall™ or other separator

Wet/dry sandpaper in 320, 400, and 600 grits

Buffing wheel or a soft cotton cloth

Face mold, with face about 1½" (3.8 cm) wide; make one or buy one**

Sharp blade

Pasta machine

Burnt umber acrylic paint

Stiff paintbrush

Glaze: FIMO non-water-based glaze, Future floor finish, or Flecto Diamond Varathane Elite floor polish

Cyanoacrylate glue

**See Stamps and Molds section of book.*

1. Cut a 1" (2.5 cm) circle from the 2¾" (7 cm) top circle for a frame to hold the jewel.

2. The jewel is fastened into the top with a textured strip of clay.

3. Making a Jewel. Mix a small amount of copper clay into some translucent. You will need enough to make a ball that will just fit into the 1" (2.5 cm) opening you cut in the frame. Form the ball, fitting it carefully to the center opening of your frame. Remove the ball from the frame, and set the frame aside. Roll out a thin snake of black clay and, with a needle tool, indent it along its length so that it appears as if there are small black beads going the length of it (see Photo 2). Cut the snake to the size that will fit around the middle of the ball. This forms a sort of bezel. Bake the ball with the bezel attached. This is the jewel for the top of the paperweight; it will sit down into the frame you have made. Let cool, then sand and buff to a high shine. Set aside.

4. Making the Faces

a. Roll out some copper clay on the thickest setting of the pasta machine. Roll it through the machine a number of times, until the surface is shiny and coppery. Cut out four squares that are approximately 3" × 3" (7.5 cm × 7.5 cm). Coat the face mold with Armorall or another separator. Lay a square into the mold, and with the smooth, rounded end of a paintbrush or other tool, press the clay into the recessed areas of the mold. Add small dollops of clay to the deep areas to reinforce the face.

b. Carefully remove the clay. You now have a masklike image protruding from your square of clay. Make a total of four of these, and then trim them to fit around the sides of your waste clay base made in Step 1 (Photo 3). There should be a flat area of ½" (1 cm), which the decorative bands will cover, between the raised areas of the faces. Smooth all the edges. Bake for 45 minutes and let cool.

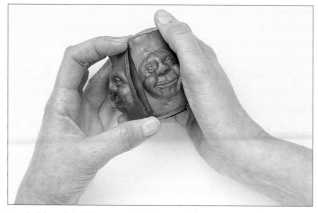

3. Add molded faces to the base of the paperweight.

5. Sanding and Antiquing the Faces and Base

a. Sand all the way around the sides of the paperweight, starting with a 320 grit, then 400, and ending with 600. Be careful not to sand off any of the facial features. Lightly buff the surface on a buffing wheel, or with a soft cotton cloth.

b. Antique the base using burnt umber acrylic paint. Use a stiff paintbrush and dab the paint firmly against the surface so that it goes into all of the recessed areas. Wipe off all of the surface paint, leaving paint only in the recessed areas. The antiquing not only gives the piece an Old World look, but it also defines the features. Let the paint dry thoroughly and then rebuff, or coat with glaze for a very shiny look.

6. Making the Textured Pieces for the Sides of the Faces.

You now need to make 4 textured pieces that will frame the faces. Using black clay, roll out a sheet on the #1 setting of the pasta machine (⅛", 3.2 mm thick). Texture one side of the sheet by pressing it against a rubber stamp, stamp mold, or texture sheet. Cut out 4 strips, each about 3" tall (or the height of your base plus a bit) × ½" wide (7.5 × 1 cm). Gild the raised textured areas with copper powder, and fit one

4. Gilded and textured strips of clay hide the seams between faces.

piece between each pair of faces, curving the ends under and over the base (Photo 4).

7. Bezel Ring. Set the jeweled frame on top of the base. Make a bezel type ring with black clay like the one you made around the small jewel ball. It should run around the entire top edge of the piece. Press it firmly against the edge (Photo 5). A bit of Translucent Liquid Sculpey will help it to adhere to the baked clay.

5. Another strip of clay is added to hold the top onto the base.

8. Finishing. Roll out a sheet of black clay on the thickest setting of the pasta machine (⅛" or 3.2 mm), and then cut out a circle the size of the bottom of the paperweight from it. Using liquid clay, fit the bottom onto the piece. Bake the entire piece for 30 minutes and let cool completely. After baking, coat the textured strips alongside the faces with some glaze to protect the powder. Gently hand buff the surface of the jewel, the bezels, and the faces. Your paperweight is now ready to hold down all those important papers on your desk.

LUMINOUS TILES

Designer
Sarajane Helm

Sarajane has been designing and selling her jewelry, teaching polymer clay classes, and writing magazine articles on the subject for many years. She has developed an extremely simple yet effective method of making tiny textured tiles, which can be used for many projects, including the little box shown. These luminous tiles measure ¾" (2 cm) square. Making these tiles is also a wonderful way to create swatches to remind you of how background colors appear when gilded with various colors of mica powders. Reminder: Wear a mask when working with powders.

MATERIALS

For Tiles:

Polymer clay in a variety of colors for the tile swatches, or black*

Mica powders in as many colors as possible

Rubber stamps

Ruler

Sharp blade

*The tile box shown was made with black clay.

Pasta machine

Clay-compatible glaze such as the ones by FIMO or Sculpey, or Flecto Varathane Diamond Elite, or Future acrylic floor finish

To Make the Box You Will Also Need:

Cardboard or other box

Translucent Liquid Sculpey

Sobo™ or other good white glue

Tiles

1. Roll out each tile clay color on the #3 setting (³⁄₃₂", 2.4 mm) of the pasta machine. Use different rubber stamps to impress designs into the surface of each sheet of clay. You can use commercial stamps or design your own patterns and have a stamp maker turn them into stamps and a matrix mold (see Techniques section of book).

2. Use a ruler to measure, and cut each sheet of color into ¾" (2 cm) squares with a sharp blade. Gently gild the top and edges of each square with mica powder (Photo 1). Vary how you do these — coat orange squares with gold, red/silver, red/blue, and so forth.

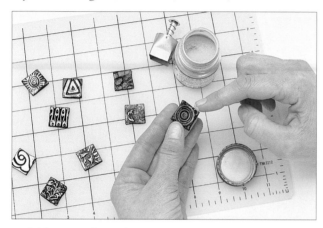

1. Gilding raw tiles with mica powders.

3. If you plan to use these as swatches, place them on your baking surface and bake at the manufacturer's recommended temperature and time. Let cool. Coat each square with one of the clay-compatible glazes to protect the powders on the surface. If you wish to use these for a box, see next instructions and don't bake yet.

Tiled Box

1. To tile a box, first cover the outside of the box with a coat of white glue and let dry.

2. Prepare the tiles as above, but do not bake yet. Set the tiles in place on top of the dry glue (Photo 2), cutting some to fit, where necessary. The inside of the box can be left plain or given a thin coating of liquid clay before baking. Bake and cool the box, and coat the tile squares with glaze.

2. Positioning tiles on the box.

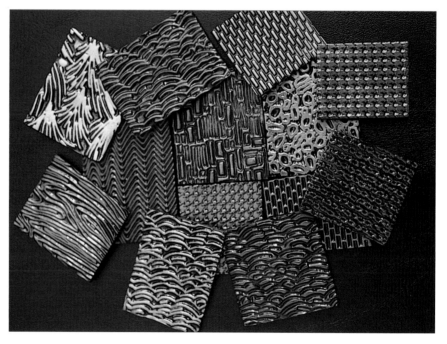

Some textured and gilded tiles show what can be done.

TWINKLE LIGHT SLEEVES

Designer
Susan Hyde

Susan is a Seattle, Washington, polymer clay artist whose fanciful and colorful work is a delight to the eye. She has a degree in graphic design and has worked for many years as a designer and production artist. She has developed a unique method of mixing layers of clay to create intricate patterns for her work.

Susan's Twinkle Light Sleeves are simple to make, yet they add a sense of whimsy and color to a string of tiny lights. They can be made using just about any form of surface technique. "Any Skinner blend will work," says Susan. (See instructions in the section of the book on Skinner blends before starting.)

MATERIALS

Polymer clay in colors of your choice, including translucent and a few colors, about 2 oz (56 g) of each

Sharp blade

Pasta machine or acrylic roller

Pencil or dowel the same width as a pencil

String of mini lights

1. Make a Skinner blend shaded sheet of clay in the color combinations of your choice. Cut or fold the shaded sheet to divide it in sixths, and stack them into a loaf cane so that you get stripes or zigzags or any pleasing placement of colors from the side view (Photo 1, right back). Slice off a piece from the side of the loaf, cut the sliced piece in half (Photo 1, center), and run each half through the pasta machine on the #4 setting (5/64", 2 mm). To save some of your patterned clay, you can roll a #4 layer of translucent clay, lay a patterned slice on top, and run both the colored and translucent sheets through the pasta machine together on the #4 setting. Cut pieces for each light sleeve from the clay you just rolled; these should be about 1½ × 2" (3.8 × 5 cm) each.

2. Coil each sleeve piece around a pencil or a dowel and bend the edges out for a flower effect (Photo 2). Slip off the pencils, lay the sleeves on a nest of polyester stuffing, and bake. While the clay is still fairly warm, loosen the coil so that the clay is not sticking to itself. Let cool.

3. Wrap a sleeve around each light on a string of mini-lights (Photo 3). Plug in and turn on. Eureka! Perfect lighting for all sorts of occasions. Once you see how these look when lit up, you'll think of all kinds of colorful patterns for them. Plain colored sheets of clay can be used for these or, if you prefer, make a sheet and cover it with cane slices that are quite small in diameter. Or try texturing the clay with various things, such as rubber stamps or plastic texture sheets.

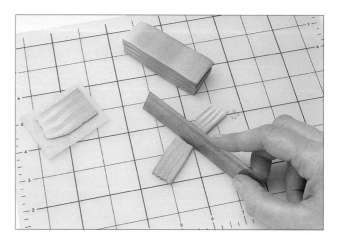

1. Stacked clay (back). Sliced-off side piece is cut in half (center). A sliced-off piece after being run through pasta machine, resting on translucent clay (left).

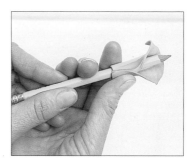

2. Clay is wrapped around the end of pencil to form the sleeve shape.

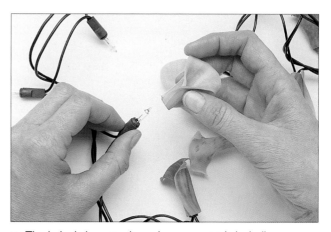

3. The baked sleeve is slipped onto a mini light bulb.

KALEIDOSCOPE

Designer
Dotty McMillan

each back in time and see if you remember those amazing tubes shaped like a telescope that displayed colorful wonders when you held them up to a light and looked through them. Incredible shimmering patterns would move and change and reform like magic as you watched. Children everywhere, along with many adults, found hours of pleasure with them.

Sir David Brewster is the person we have to thank for these treasures. When he invented them in 1816, he had no idea what joy he had given the world. Today, the old scopes are priceless collectibles and many of the new ones are high-priced museum pieces. Why not make your own kaleidoscope? It will give you hours of pure delight once it's completed. These days, kaleidoscope patterns are used not only for pleasure, but also as aids to artists, as stress reducers, and as tools in color therapy.

The directions here are for a very simple kaleidoscope. If you enjoy making them, you may want to advance to more sophisticated ones.

MATERIALS

Empty Pringles™ potato chip container and its plastic lid or similar cardboard cylinder about 3" wide (7.5 cm) and 9" (23 cm) long

Clear plastic or Plexiglas™ sheet, .03" (7 mm) thick, large enough to cut three circles to fit inside your cylinder

Polymer clay:

Black (for base color) or color of your choice, 4 oz (112 g)

White, ecru, translucent, and pearl Premo! Sculpey, about 1 oz (28 g) of each

Small pieces of various opaque colors for decorations

Translucent Liquid Sculpey

Three pieces of mirror, each 2" (5 cm) x 8¾" (22.2 cm)*

Packing such as bubble-wrap, batting, Styrofoam chips, soft cloth, etc.

Small strip of corrugated cardboard, about 1/2" × 8¾" (1 × 22 cm)

Masking or duct tape

Craft knife

Glue

Molds: Commercial ones or homemade ones of flowers, leaves, butterflies, shells, faces**

Acrylic paint: Burnt sienna (optional)

Wet/dry sandpaper

Buffing equipment or cloth

For viewing: Small bits of colored glass, translucent and transparent beads, bright colored yarns cut into 1" to 2" (2 to 5 cm) pieces, dried flowers, feathers, or any other small objects with interesting shapes and colors

*Most glass and mirror shops will do the cutting for you if you don't want to try it yourself.
**See section of book on Rubber Stamps and Molds.

1. Clean the potato chip residue from the inside of the tube if necessary. Use a sharp craft knife to make a hole in the center of the metal end of the tube large enough to see through, about ½" (1 cm). Roll out a sheet of black clay on the #4 setting (5⁄64", 2 mm) of the pasta machine. The sheet width should be the outer diameter of your cylinder times 3.14 (pi). The sheet length should be the height of the cylinder minus the cap overlap. You can leave the black clay plain or texture it. Wrap all of the tube in black clay, except the edge where the end cap will cover, and butt the clay seams together neatly (Photo 1). If you don't leave a clay-free

edge for the end cap, it will not fit on the tube when your kaleidoscope is completed. If you don't have an end cap, cover the edge with clay also. Cut a circle of clay for the end with the viewing hole, and add it on, cutting a hole in the clay also. (Photo 2 shows the viewing end of the finished kaleidoscope.)

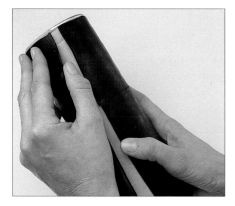

1. Potato chip can is covered with base clay.

2. View of eyepiece, showing hole cut in clay and container for viewing.

2. Mix translucent clay with small amounts of opaque clay to make a variety of tinted translucents for decorations. Peach, pink, pale blue, light yellow, soft green, and lavender all work well against the black base on the tube.

3. Set out the molds you plan to use. If you want to sculpt the pieces yourself instead, draw them out first and keep the drawings handy. Begin making the various pieces such as flowers, leaves, faces, and shells, and placing them onto the black clay on the tube. Keep checking the way your colors are placed. Make sure there aren't too many of any one color in any one area. This is a rather Zen experience. Let your instincts guide you. Cluster some flowers and leaves, or shells, etc., together and leave some of the black clay showing between other clusters. Don't try to rush this step. Take your time and make sure the arrangements are pleasing (Photo 3). Put a very small dab of Translucent Liquid Sculpey on the back of each piece to make certain it will adhere to the base clay when baking. However, don't use too much of the liquid clay or your pieces will slide around.

4. When the kaleidoscope is done to your liking, bake it while it is lying on a nest of polyester stuffing, or standing on end if your oven is tall enough, and let it cool completely.

5. Wet-sand the entire surface of the clay, but do not submerge in water as you do not want to get the cardboard tube wet. Just wet the sandpaper slightly before sanding. Use wet fingers or a damp cloth to wipe off the residue left on the piece by sanding. Buff the piece using a buffing wheel, Dremel tool, or soft cotton cloth.

6. Antique the baked clay with burnt sienna acrylic paint if you wish. Dab with a stiff brush to get the paint into all of the recesses. Use your hands to smear the paint all over the entire piece. Wash and dry your hands. With a clean piece of cloth or paper towels, wipe off any excess until you like the look. This will give the piece the patina of having aged. It will also make the details in the sculp-

3. Molded shapes are added to the base clay.

tural type pieces stand out. Buff up the shine again when the piece is completely dry.

7. Cut out two circular pieces of the clear plastic or Plexiglas that are the diameter of the inside of the tube. Glue one of the circles all the way inside the tube to the metal bottom with the eyehole. This is to cover the eyepiece and protect the eye of anyone using the kaleidoscope.

8. Be sure your mirror pieces are clean. Use a good window cleaner. Lay them with the reflective side down on your work surface, about ⅛" (3 mm) apart. Cut three pieces of tape, each 8" (20 cm) in length. Lay these across backs of the mirrors, perpendicular to

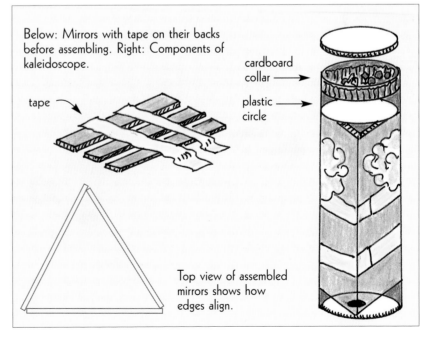

Below: Mirrors with tape on their backs before assembling. Right: Components of kaleidoscope.

tape

cardboard collar

plastic circle

Top view of assembled mirrors shows how edges align.

their length, with the excess tape hanging over one edge. Fold the mirrors into a triangular prism shape and use the excess tape to bind the mirrors in place. Be sure that the edge of each mirror touches the front surface of the adjacent mirror all around the triangle.

9. Carefully insert the prism of mirrors into the decorated tube and add packing material such as batting or Styrofoam chips on all three sides as you do (Photo 4). You want them to be snugly packed and have no wiggle or other movement inside the tube. The mirrors should end up being flush with the viewing end of the tube.

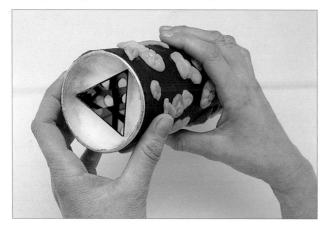

4. Mirrors are packed inside the tube.

10. Place the second circle of clear plastic on top of the mirrors' ends. Take the strip of corrugated cardboard and form it into a collar that fits around the inside of the tube end above the second plastic circle. This makes the chamber where your kaleidoscope objects will go. Fill this chamber about two-thirds of the way full with such things as small transparent glass and plastic pieces, colored yarns, etc. (Photo 5).

5. Decorative items are placed in the object chamber, and the cap is put on.

11. Snap on the plastic cap that came with the potato chip container. If you don't have one, cut and glue in a third clear plastic circle. Hold the scope to a light source, turn it slowly, and watch the wonderful patterns form.

Variations: You can take off the cap and remove the objects and cardboard strip from the chamber and use the scope to view the world around you. This makes it into a world scope, which you can use to view everything around in patterns.

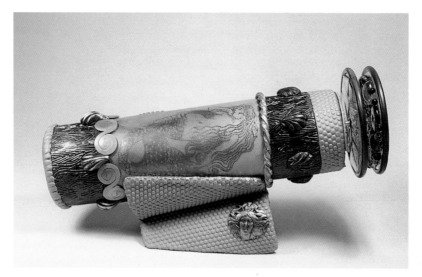

Blue Water, Deep kaleidoscope by the author.

CHINESE GOOD LUCK LANTERN

Designer
Cassie Doyan

Cassie Doyan, a very active member of the polymer clay community, designed this striking lantern. The central motif is the Chinese symbol for good luck. The translucent clay resembles frosted glass or paper. A tranquil light glows forth when the lantern is lit. The lantern is a great way to add a special touch to any room. It can easily be wired, using a lighting kit purchased at a ceramic supply shop (small bulbs only, please). Or you may simply place a votive candle inside for a softer light. The lantern is designed for indoor use only.

MATERIALS

Polymer clay:

    Black Premo! Sculpey or FIMO Classic, 1 lb (454 g)

    Translucent Premo! Sculpey or FIMO Classic, 1 lb (454 g)

Wire armature mesh, about 17 × 12" (43 × 30 cm)

Light green acrylic paint

Pasta machine

Sharp knife

Wax paper or tracing paper

Scissors for cutting mesh

1. Making the Templates. Trace or photocopy two copies of the pattern for the side of the lantern. From the patterns, cut out one template (Template 1) from paper or cardboard, cutting around the outside edges of the black design only to make a 5 × 5" square (12.7 × 12.7 cm). For the second template (Template 2), cut away the white parts of the template paper inside and outside the design, leaving only the black parts. Template 2 will be the template for the lantern frame. (Set the Chinese characters aside for now.)

2. Cutting the "Glass" Panels. Roll out translucent clay on the #1 setting (⅛", 3.2 mm) of the pasta machine so you have a sheet larger than 5 × 5". Tape a piece of wax paper over Template 1 to protect it. Lay the sheet of translucent clay over Template 1 and trim the translucent clay to fit the 5 × 5" square pattern of Template 1 to make one side of the lantern's "glass" (Photo 1). Repeat three times for the remaining sides. Important: On two opposite edges of two of the lantern "glasses," trim the clay approximately ⅛" (3 mm) in from the template's edge. This will help fit the lantern's sides together after the sides are baked. Carefully remove the translucent clay "glass" from the template each time you make one. Set them aside.

3. Making the Frames. Roll out black clay on the #1 setting (⅛", 3 mm) of the pasta machine. Place Template 2 over the sheet of black clay and use the template as a guide to cut the black clay to match the frame pattern (Photo 2). When done, slide it off the template onto a sheet of wax paper. Using Template 2

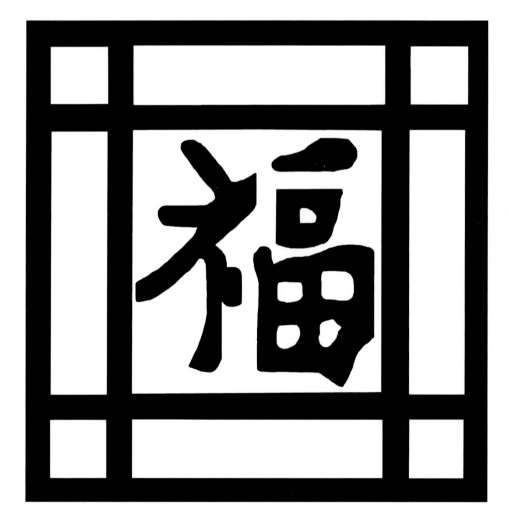

Pattern for lantern side, at 100%.

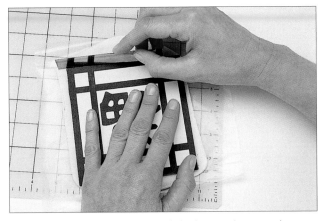

1. Cut out the "glass" portion of the lantern from translucent clay.

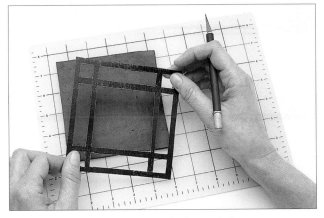

2. Use the template to cut out the lantern's frame.

again, cut another frame from another sheet of black clay and cut it apart in strips. Cut wire mesh pieces to fit the strips of clay and lay each piece of wire strip onto a strip of clay (Photo 3). Put the clay strip with wire mesh on top of the first black clay frame, sandwiching the mesh between the two layers of clay. Do this for the whole frame. This will add needed strength to the frame of the lantern. Gently close the seams together with your fingers to seal and hide any of the wire mesh. Don't smooth the clay too much. You want the lantern to have an ancient, weathered look. This completes one frame side. Make 3 more frame sides the same way.

4. Carefully lift a lantern frame side made in Step 3, and place it on top of the translucent "glass" square.

Press down on the black clay and make sure it adheres to the translucent clay. Form the good luck characters by hand with pieces of black clay. Gently press the character pieces into the center of one translucent square of the lantern (Photo 4).

5. Repeat attaching the frames and characters to the other three lantern "glasses" (Step 4) and bake, with the lantern as yet unassembled, according to the clay manufacturer's instructions. I generally bake the sides for one-half hour, placing the clay in the cold oven and turning it on so that the clay slowly preheats to 250°F (121°C) within the 30-minute period. After the clay is finished baking, I let it cool in the oven to prevent any cracking.

3. Reinforce the frame with wire.

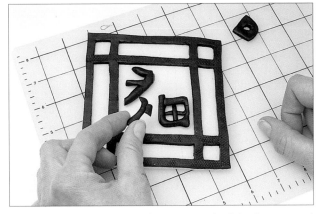

4. Shape and add Chinese characters to the "glass" portion of the lantern.

6. Once the clay is cooled, bring two lantern sides together at a 90-degree angle. Press translucent Premo! clay into the adjoining edges of the inside (Photo 5). Press black clay into the adjoining edges of the outside so that the two sides will adhere to each other. Repeat with the remaining two lantern sides; then join the two sets of sides together with translucent and black clay. Bake and let cool.

7. To make the top, roll out black clay on the #1 setting (⅛", 3.2 mm) of the pasta machine. Cut out a 7 × 7" (18 × 18 cm) square. Trim wire mesh to fit; then place another layer of black clay on top of the mesh, sandwiching the mesh between the two sheets of black clay. Bake and cool.

8. To attach the top of the lantern to the sides, put a layer of translucent clay along the top edge of the sides. Put the top on, making sure the top overlaps equally on all sides. Gently press the top onto the sides. Then press black clay into the outer edges where the top joins the sides, and press translucent clay into the edges where they join inside the lantern. Bake the entire lantern. Cool.

9. To complete the lantern, lightly sponge light green acrylic paint onto the black clay to give it the look of an aged patina. Use a low-wattage bulb to light up the lantern, not a candle.

5. Reinforce the corners of the lantern with extra clay.

This lantern can be created with many different looks. For instance, the top and frames of the lantern could be made with Granitex™ stone colors of clay or FIMO™ granite colors to give it a look of stone. A mixture of clays can give it the appearance of faux jade. Coat black clay with Pearl-Ex mica powders or Eberhard/Faber Pulvers (powders) to make it resemble metal. An assortment of central motifs can be used to personalize your lantern. The possibilities are limitless.

SEGMENTED BRACELET

Designer
Dotty McMillan

This is a fun and easy bracelet to make. You can use just about any surface technique you like, or combine different techniques for a "sampler" bracelet. Mokume gane, photo transfers, canes, on-lay and inlay, and impressions all work well. For this project, I've chosen black-and-white transfers on white clay with black backings, but you can choose any colors or techniques you like.

MATERIALS

Cardboard

Tape measure

Polymer clay:

    Black, 2 oz (56 g)

    White, 2 oz (56 g)

    Translucent Liquid Sculpey

Transfer images*

Needle tool

Pasta machine or roller

Sharp blade

Good quality narrow jewelry elastic cord

Filler beads to go between segments (optional)**

Cyanoacrylate glue

Wet/dry sandpaper in 320, 400, and 600 grits

Buffing equipment

*See Black-and-White Transfers section of book.
**You can make the beads of clay or buy them.

1. Measuring. The first thing to figure is the size of the bracelet. Segments that are 1½" (4 cm) tall work for most people, although they can be taller or shorter, depending on your taste. The width will depend on the size of the wrist. With a tape measure, measure around the wrist that will wear the bracelet. Don't pull the tape measure really tight. Leave a little play in it. Subtract 1" (2.5 cm) from this measure. For instance, if the wrist measures 7½" (19 cm), subtract the inch for a total of 6½" (16.5 cm). Now, divide that total by 5 (the number of segments). The result will be the width you will make each segment (in this case 1½" or 4 cm). Make a pattern the size of the segment on a piece of cardboard and cut it out.

2. Making the Bottom and Middle Layer of the Segments. There are three layers to each segment. The top layer is the one with the surface technique. The second is the layer that is cut to form channels for your elastic cord to go through. The third layer is the back piece of the segment, which will end up touching your wrist. Roll out your black clay on the #3 setting (³⁄₃₂", 2.4 mm) of the pasta machine. Cut out ten pieces using the cardboard pattern you made. Five will be for the backing layer. Five will be for the middle layer. Trim away about ½" (1 cm) on each of the middle-layer pieces and cut the five narrowed middle-layer pieces into 3 parts. Lay the 3 cut pieces onto a backing piece of black clay as shown in Photo 1, leaving channels for the elastic. That completes the bottom and middle layers for one segment. Prepare the remaining 4 backing pieces the same way. Set these aside.

3. Making the Top Layer. Decide which transfers you will use for your top layer. Make a sheet of white clay for the top layer that is approximately the same thickness as the #3 setting (³⁄₃₂", 2.4 mm) on the pasta machine. Cut out five pieces from this sheet, using the segment pattern you made in Step 1 as a template. These are the pieces for your top layer, or decorative layer, of the bracelet. Lay a transfer onto each of the five pieces and follow the instructions for Black-and-White Transfers in the Techniques section of the book, including baking.

4. Joining the Layers. For each segment, place a top piece onto the other two layers you joined in Step 2, and gently press the layers together. Since your transfer layer has been baked, you can use some Liquid Sculpey to help the layers bond together. If you don't have liquid clay, bake the pieces together and check to make certain they are well attached. If not, snap them off and glue them back on. For a catch, make a small bar out of clay with two holes going through it (see Photo 2, upper left). Bake and let cool.

5. Sanding. Sand and buff all five segments, except for the top layers with the transfers. Choose or make filler beads to go between the segments that are ¼" (0.6 cm) wide with holes large enough to accommodate the jewelry elastic.

6. Assembling. Lay the segments out in a line with two filler beads between each piece, one next to each channel. Fold a piece of elastic in half and feed an elastic end through a channel in the first segment and then through a filler bead (Photo 2). Do the same with the other elastic end. Continue doing this with the remaining segments and beads. At the end of the last segment, feed the ends of the elastic through the two holes of the bar you baked (Photo 3). Snug the elastic up and tie a knot linking the two ends. Secure the knot with a dab of glue. Snip off the excess elastic.

The bar on one side of the bracelet will fit through the loop of elastic at the other end of the bracelet and form a catch. You can fasten and unfasten the bracelet each time you use it, or you can fasten the catch and, because of the elastic, just slip the bracelet on and off.

There are many variations to this type of bracelet. You can use segments that are not all the same width, as long as you get the total bracelet dimensions correct. You can make the layers a little thinner and then lay each piece over a rounded surface when baking so that each has a slight curve to it, which makes a rounder looking bracelet. You can make the bracelet with more but narrower segments and eliminate the filler beads. It all depends upon the look you want.

1. Middle layers are cut so there are channels for the cords. At right, bottom and middle layers together.

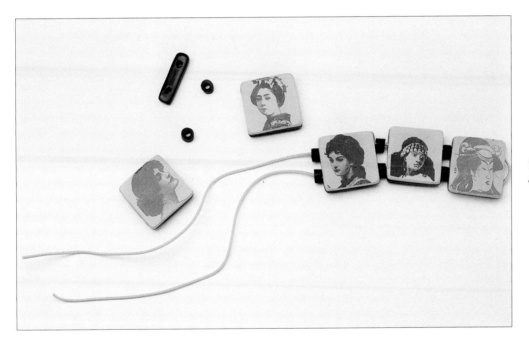

2. Partially strung bracelet and catch (upper left).

3. Closeup of end, before elastic is tied.

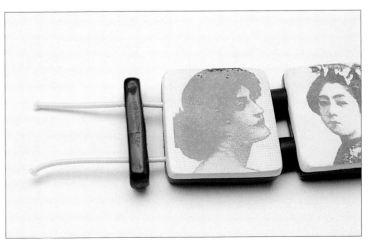

BLUE MASK

Designer: Dotty McMillan
based on an original design by
Susan Bradshaw

Susan Bradshaw says she has been "a maker" all of her life. Polymer clay has become her material of choice because of its color and pattern possibilities. This mask is based on one of hers. What fun you can have making these masks for costume affairs, to decorate your walls, for the kids, or for sale. Susan's method is easy. You will find yourself coming up with many variations to suit your needs.

MATERIALS

Polymer clay:

    Scrap clay for base, 8 to 10 oz (228 to 285 g)

    Blue clay or color of your choice, 4 to 6 oz (114 to 171 g)

    Premade canes or other embellishments*

Acrylic roller or brayer

WireForm® or other wire mesh armature screen, about 10" × 10" (25 × 25 cm)

Person who will lend you his/her face

*See Making Canes section of book.

Drinking straws

A light cloth, waxed paper, or cold cream for covering the person's face before applying clay

Marker

Heavy scissors

Drill and small drill bit (⅛" or .3 cm)

Strong cord or ribbon

Sharp blade

Craft knife

Polyester stuffing

1. Making the Mask Base

a. Roll out two sheets of scrap clay on the thickest setting of the pasta machine. Make these as wide as your machine will allow. Trim them to 5 × 10" (13 × 25 cm). Place them side by side on a piece of armature screen. Join the long edges of the clay and roll the screen into the clay using an acrylic roller or brayer. The clay side will become the inside of your mask (Photo 1).

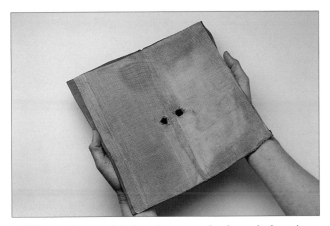

1. Wire mesh was added to the waste clay base, before shaping the mask on a face. Nose holes were cut.

b. You need another person to be your model. Cover the model's face with a light cloth, waxed paper, or coat it with cold cream to protect the skin. If the mask-wearer will be wearing glasses underneath, leave them on while you mold the clay so the shape will conform to them. Mark where the nose holes will be, lift the clay off the face, and cut holes so that your model can breathe while you work. Replace the clay over the face, with the wire side out. Begin molding the clay and wire until you get the basic shape of your mask. Be careful, as the wire edges can be very sharp.

c. Place the molded clay with wire-side down in a nest of polyester stuffing in the oven and bake for 15 to 20 minutes at the temperature recommended by the manufacturer of the clay. Let it cool completely.

d. Place the baked clay piece on your work surface and mark a line all the way around it to show where to trim off any edges you don't need. Cut along this line with heavy kitchen scissors or a sharp craft knife. Mark the location for the eye holes and cut them out with the craft knife. Cut them slightly larger than the final size you desire.

e. If you prefer, you can tug away the wire screen, leaving only clay in your mask base. You have now made the base form for your mask; it is ready for embellishment.

2. Finishing the Mask

a. There are many different ways to complete the mask. These directions are for the Blue Mask. Make any changes you want in order to form the image you have in mind, using the basic instructions. For example, you can cover the entire mask with another sheet of clay which has been embellished before you apply it. Or you could lay individual slices of canes over the base.

b. For the Blue Mask, roll out sheets of blue clay as you did with the scrap clay in Step 1, and cover the mask base with a sheet of blue clay. Be sure to bring this layer down around the edges of the mask, the edges of the eye holes, and the edges of the nose holes. Build up any facial features you wish. When doing this, remember that flat angular planes will read as round from a distance and round features will look flat from a distance. If you wish to add cane slices to the mask, now is the time to do that (Photo 2). Bake the piece for 30 minutes and let cool. Drill a hole in the right and left side at about ear height and about ½" (1 cm) in from the edge. Attach ties to the mask so it will stay on your head. Put on your mask and have fun.

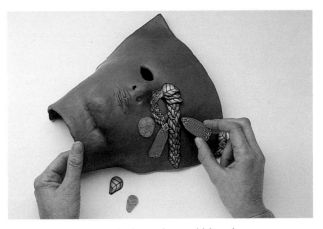

2. Cane slices are applied to a layer of blue clay.

CHUNKY ART DECO BRACELET

Designer
Dotty McMillan

I f you have ever had a passion for those cuff bracelets made of Bakelite in the late 1920s and 1930s, this is the project for you. The bracelets can be made in any color combination, but check out some color books on Bakelite for more inspiration.

1. Roll out three different colors of clay, or three shades of the same color, on the #2 setting (⁷⁄₆₄", 2.8 mm) of the pasta machine. From each of the colors, cut one strip that is 8½" × 1½" (21.5 × 4 cm). Decide which strip will be the top layer of your bracelet and which will be the inside. (Set the third sheet aside for now. It will be used for the circle.) Stack one strip on top of the other and gently press together.
2. Impress your third color sheet with a rubber stamp,

a mold made from a stamp, or any other item that will leave a pattern in the clay that resembles carving. From this impressed sheet, cut out a circle that is slightly wider than 1½" (4 cm) diameter, the width of your stacked strips. Place the circle in the center of the top strip (see Photo 1). The circle is the centerpiece of your bracelet.
3. Impress designs on the leftover portions of the sheet of clay that you used for the inside of the bracelet, and

MATERIALS

Polymer clay:

    Premo! Sculpey or FIMO in your choice of three colors or 3 shades of the same color, 4 oz (114 g) total

    Translucent Liquid Sculpey (optional)

    Waste clay for making bracelet mandrel (if needed), 8 oz (228 g)*

Bracelet mandrel, oval shaped (or make your own out of waste clay)*

Rubber stamps or rubber stamp molds

Cutters in various shapes

Wet/dry sandpaper in 320, 400, and 600 grits

Soft cotton cloth or other equipment for buffing

Acrylic paint or oil paint: burnt sienna or burnt umber, or color of your choice for antiquing (optional)**

Oil paint for antiquing (optional)

Pasta machine

Sharp blade

*A bracelet mandrel is basically a tapering metallic cylinder shape (see photo) to hold and help shape bracelets to the right size. If you don't have one, make one out of waste clay and bake it before starting the bracelet.
**Use if you wish to antique and accent your faux carving. Or you could use Translucent Liquid Sculpey and oil paint.

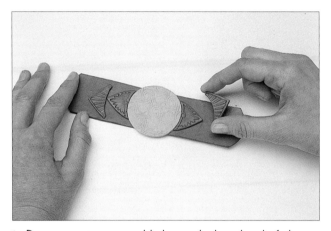

1. Decorative pieces are added onto the base band of clay.

from the same sheet cut out triangles, diamonds, circles, or squares that are about one-third the size of your center circle. Place one of these shapes on either side of your centerpiece (Photo 1). Press all of the added pieces gently to make certain they are adhered to the stacked strips.

4. Measure the arm of the wearer with a string or measuring tape and mark the place where this string fits on the bracelet mandrel. Leave about ½" (1 cm) extra in addition to the circumference of the person's arm. Gently lift the assembled bracelet and wrap it around the bracelet mandrel at the desired size. You

can adjust it slightly by trimming the ends of the strip or stretching the piece a bit. The ends of the strip should be touching each other. Press them just enough to ensure that they will hold, but not so hard that they will be totally fixed after baking. You will be pulling or cutting them apart, if necessary, after the piece is baked and cooled. Check to make sure each of the added pieces is firmly attached to the stacked strips of clay. If desired, add contrast to the designs by gently painting with some Translucent Liquid Sculpey tinted with oil paint (or wait until the piece is baked and then use acrylic paint to antique it).

5. Bake the bracelet on the mandrel. If your oven is tall enough, stand the mandrel upright. If the oven isn't that tall, lay the mandrel lengthwise and prop the ends up on something so that the bracelet doesn't touch the baking surface. Two metal cookie cutters work well for this. Bake at the recommended temperature and let cool. When cool, gently work the bracelet off the mandrel (Photo 2). You may need a small tool of some kind to encourage the release.

6. Once the bracelet is cool, it's time to remove all of the sharp and/or rough edges. Go over the entire piece with the 320 grit wet/dry sandpaper. Be sure you sand the inside of the bracelet as well as the outside. Caution: Don't sand the faux carved pieces too hard, as this will remove the impressions. Just lightly sand in a circular motion to break the surface tension for ease of antiquing and buffing. As you sand, concentrate more pressure on the sharp edges of the bracelet. You want to round these off. Go to the 400 grit sandpaper and repeat the above steps. Do the same with the 600 grit. Briskly buff the whole piece with a soft piece of cotton cloth.

2. Gently remove the bracelet from the mandrel after baking.

Troubleshooting: If you discover your bracelet is too large for the wrist it's intended for, trim off some from each end with your sharp blade; then sand and finish it like the rest of the bracelet. Wrap the bracelet tightly with cotton string, pulling the two ends tightly together. Rebake for about 10 minutes, remove from the oven, and check to make sure the two ends are still evenly together. Drop the piece into a bowl of ice water and let it sit for about ten minutes. It should hold its new shape and size with no problem.

7. If you didn't use the Translucent Liquid Sculpey and oil paint to antique your bracelet, this is the time to use the acrylic paints to do that. See the Antiquing part of the Techniques section of the book.

8. If you have a buffing wheel, buff the surfaces to a lovely shine. If you don't have a buffing wheel, leave your piece as is, buff it a bit more with the cotton cloth, or coat the surfaces with one or two layers of Future floor finish or another glaze.

Two more bracelet ideas.

CHUNKY ART DECO BRACELET

HATPINS OR LAPEL PINS

Designer
Dotty McMillan*

You may think of hat pins as charming but outdated items from a distant past. You couldn't be more wrong! Give these wonderful old-style adornments a new life by embellishing them with polymer clay goodies. Even if you don't wear hats, they can be renamed "lapel pins" and worn on a suit jacket or sweater. You will get a lot of interest and compliments, whichever way you wear them.

MATERIALS

Small amounts of polymer clay, canes, etc., for the techniques you want to use

Stick pins about 5" (12.5 cm) long with clutches and small- to medium-sized heads (available at most bead stores)**

Cyanoacrylate glue

Loop or eye pins and flathead pins for dangles (optional)

Small beads or canes for dangles (optional)

Glaze or antiquing materials

Regular clay tools

*Photo on this page shows hatpins by many artists.
**Longer stick pins are okay for hats, but are more difficult to use on lapels.

Decide what types of pins you want to make. Pins made of colorful canes, luminous translucent clays, mokume gane, polished faux jade or other stones, carved or molded figures, and ethnic patterns are among the many choices. (See photographs and also Techniques part of book for ideas and supplies. The hatpin being made in the photos was made with cane slices over white clay.)

1. Polymer clay does not adhere to metal. The flat head on the stick pin helps somewhat to keep the pin and clay together, but it's not enough for real stability, so before applying clay, give the metal head of the stick pin a thin coat of glue, but don't let it dry. Apply a tiny ball of clay and bake (Photo 1). Next, apply the rest of the clay, using the technique you have chosen.

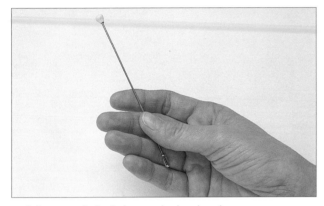

1. Bake a tiny ball of clay on the head end.

2. If you are adding a dangle at the top of the pin, be sure you insert a loop pin into the unbaked clay on the stick pin. Cut the the straight part of the loop pin to double the length that will be covered in clay and then fold the loop pin not quite in half so that it forms a slightly lopsided U. Slowly press the rounded bottom of the U into the clay, until only the looped portion of the pin is showing, and then press the clay firmly around it. This will insure that the loop pin stays in the clay after baking.

3. Make beads for the dangles, if desired.

4. Bake the pin, without the clutch, on polyester stuffing, and bake any clay beads you want to make. When cool, glaze or antique as desired.

5. For the dangle: String the beads onto a flathead pin and trim pin to size; make a loop at the end and attach it to the loop pin imbedded in the top of the hatpin.

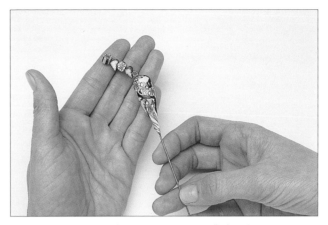

2. A dangle of cane beads, strung on a flathead pin, attached to the top of the hatpin.

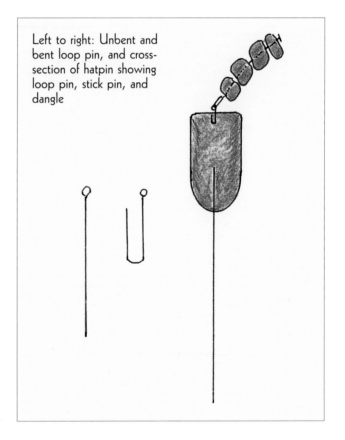

Left to right: Unbent and bent loop pin, and cross-section of hatpin showing loop pin, stick pin, and dangle

TINY BOOKS

Designer
Deborah Anderson

*D*eborah Anderson is a founding member of the Southbay Polymer Clay Guild in Northern California. Her 20 years of experience in pottery and leather have influenced her clay designs. Deborah's wonderful polymer clay work has been seen in numerous craft magazines. Here she shows you how to make a delightful leatherlike book in a small size that will please anyone, the perfect gift for that person who loves books.

1. The Inside Pages. For each book, cut 20 to 30 pieces of paper 3" × 4" (9 × 10 cm) for pages. On one piece of paper, mark lines ½" (1 cm) from the top and ½" from the bottom and ½" in from the left side, and punch holes at the intersections of the lines on all the pieces of paper. Make sure you align the holes through all the pages.

2. Front and Back Edge. For each book cut two strips out of black leather that are 1½" × 4½" (3.8 × 11.5 cm). Fold over ¼ (0.6 cm) on the long sides of each piece so that you have nice clean edges, and glue the folded part to the back of the leather strip. Line up the holes using one of the sheets of paper as a guide, and punch 2 matching holes on each leather strip.

3. Front and Back Covers. Roll terra cotta colored clay through the pasta machine on the #5 setting (1⁄16", 1.6 mm). Place an extra piece of leather with grain side down on top of the clay, and use the acrylic roller to roll a nice, even impression of the leather onto the clay. Cut out two covers from the clay, for the front and the back of the book, each 2¾" (7 cm) wide and 4¼" (11 cm) long.

MATERIALS

Polymer clay: FIMO Classic (or other clay in similar colors)

    Terra cotta, 4 oz (112 g)

    Champagne, ½ oz (14 g)

    Black, ¼ oz (7 g)

Very thin blade

Exacto™ knife (or other craft knife)

Piece of leather with pebble or other grain, about 6" × 6" (15 × 15 cm)

Acrylic roller

Pasta machine

Paper: Enough for 30 leaves, 3" × 4" (7.5 × 10 cm)

Scissors

Steel wool pad, #000 (fine)

Rubber stamp with image

Permanent ink pad, black

Hole punch

Black leather, thin enough to sew through, about 4" × 5" (10 × 13 cm)

Needle tool

Glue

Needle, thread, and thimble or sewing machine

4. The Window Cutout on the Front Cover

a. Roll out a sheet of champagne clay on the #5 setting (¹⁄₁₆", 1.6 mm) on the pasta machine. Texture the clay with a steel wool pad to make it look like suede. Next, ink your rubber stamp with the black permanent ink pad and stamp the image onto the champagne clay. Set it aside.

b. Make a paper window template by folding a piece of paper in half and in half again. Cut out an oval shape from the paper where the folds intersect, or use whatever window shape you choose, being sure it's a little larger than the stamped design.

c. Place the paper template on top of one of the terra cotta covers, and with an Exacto knife cut out a window of the same size in the clay.

d. Roll out the black clay on the #6 setting (¹⁄₃₂", 0.8 mm), to a very thin sheet. Texture it with the pebble grain leather and cut out a frame, using the paper template you made previously to get the frame's inner dimension, and adding ⅛" (.3 cm) around the template for the outside of the frame, so it will fit just right. Place the black frame on the terra cotta front cover (Photo 1). If you like, use a needle tool to make imitation stitching lines.

e. Next, cut out a shape with the stamped image from

1. Add a frame to the opening on the front cover.

the champagne clay, but make sure the piece you cut is a little bit larger than the window you cut. Carefully place the champagne clay shape with the design centered under the opening in the terra cotta front cover, so that it fits nicely (Photo 2).

f. Place both covers on a baking surface. Bake both covers at 250°F (121°C) for one hour, and let cool.

5. Finishing the Book.
Put one long edge of a leather strip ¼" (0.6 cm) under the side of the front cover. Glue and stitch the leather to the clay on a sewing ma-

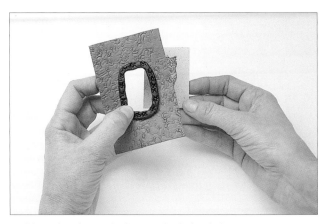

2. Place the clay with the transfer behind the opening.

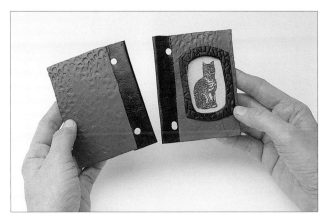

3. Front and back cover, after edge is glued on.

These books used color transfer designs and gilding.

chine or by hand with a strong needle, strong thread, and a thimble. Repeat for back cover (Photo 3).

Cut out two pieces of leather the same sizes as the covers to glue onto the insides of the covers. Gather the stacks of sheets and assemble them between the front and back covers, lining up the holes. Cut a narrow strip of leather for the lacing, lace it through the holes, and tie a bow on the front cover.

There are many ways to make miniature books. A few photos are included to spark your imagination.

Some tiny books by Deborah Anderson.

ART DECO BROOCH

Designer
Dotty McMillan

One of the most interesting design periods of the 20th century emerged in the Paris art world of 1925. Art Deco's bold geometric patterns at first shocked, then delighted people. Although it became evident in everything from wallpaper to upholstery, nowhere was it more engaging than in the jewelry of that period.

This brooch utilizes several polymer clay techniques which, when combined, offer you a chance to look back in time and yet create something entirely new.

Many Art Deco jewelry pieces were made from Bakelite, a popular early plastic that came in a variety of interesting colors: apple juice, coffee with cream, cinnamon, olive, deep caramel, milky peach, creamed corn, grass green, burnt orange, tortoise shell, cobalt, chocolate, burgundy, teal, ruby, coral, chartreuse, as well as black, white, and ivory. In this project, you are not duplicating Bakelite jewelry exactly, but part of your brooch will have a resemblance.

1. Stamping. Make or buy molds or hard plastic stamps for the dangle, pin bar, and circular parts. (If you wish, use the pendant design given here.)

2. Hanging Deco Design (Faux Bakelite)

a. Mix one walnut-sized piece of orange clay into a walnut-sized piece of translucent clay and add a ¼-pea-sized piece of black. Mix thoroughly. This should give you a burnt-orange or apple juice color. If the orange still looks a bit too saturated, add a tiny bit more of black. Mix again. Roll the clay out on the #1 setting (⅛", 3.2 mm) of the pasta machine.

MATERIALS

Polymer clay, ½ oz (14 g) of each:

    Black

    Beige/ecru

    Translucent

    Orange

Circle cutter, 2" (5 cm)

Scissors

Burnishing tool

Mold release: Armorall, talc, or cornstarch

Tracing paper and pencil

Art Deco rubber stamps or molds from the stamps* or any interesting stamp patterns you like

Colored pencils

Copy-shop copy or laser printer copy of small art deco motif such as the face given here, 1 to 1½" (2.5 to 4 cm) wide

Gold wax or Pearl-Ex metallic mica powder

Acrylic paint: burnt umber and burnt sienna

Sharp blade

Pasta machine

Pin back and two large jump rings, 12 to 14 mm circumference

Narrow plastic tubing, such as is used in a fish tank, 2" (5 cm), optional

Cord for hanging brooch (optional)

Wet/dry sandpaper in 320, 400, and 600 grits

Buffing wheel or soft cotton cloth

*See section of book on Rubber Stamps and Molds for instructions if you want to make your own. Or you could draw designs on the clay with a needle tool.

Pattern for dangle.

ing design outline from the book; cut it out of paper, and lay it on the clay. Cut the clay to the shape of the pattern (Photo 1). Make two small holes in the clay, as shown on the pattern piece, where it will attach to the circular piece with jump rings.

c. Bake the hanging piece and cool. Sand and buff the impressed side as well as the back of the piece. Lightly

b. Coat an Art Deco pattern mold or a rubber stamp for the hanging design with Armorall, talc, or cornstarch. Press the sheet of orange clay into the mold or against the rubber stamp. Press it well into the recessed areas. Gently remove the clay. If you don't have a mold, you can just draw or trace a pattern onto the clay with a needle tool. Trace out the Art Deco hang-

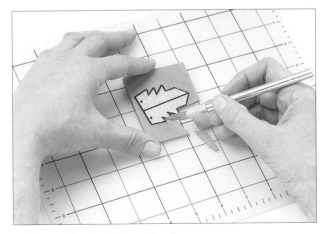

1. Cut out the dangle from the clay.

antique the hanging piece with an equal mixture of burnt umber and burnt sienna acrylic paint. Set aside.

3. Circular Centerpiece. Roll out the black clay on the #1 setting (⅛", 3.2 mm) of the pasta machine. Apply one of the mold releases to an Art Deco stamp or mold or other design piece you like, and press the clay against it. Remove carefully. Cut out the circle from the black clay, using the 2" round cutter (Photo 2). Trim off the bottom curve of the circle (see Photo 3 for shape). Make two round holes in the trimmed circle side. These holes should line up exactly with the two holes in the hanging faux Bakelite piece made earlier. Bake the circle and cool. Sand and buff. Set aside.

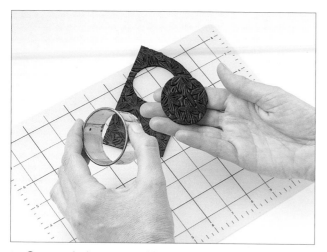

2. Cut a circle from textured black clay.

4. Pin Bar. Roll out a small piece of black clay on the #1 setting (⅛", 3.2 mm) of the pasta machine. Impress with your choice of rubber stamp or stamp mold. Using the pattern in the book as a guide, trace and cut out the pin bar from the clay. Bake and cool. The pin bar will be glued to the back of the black circle piece you have made. You will then glue your pin back to the back of the bar. Seen from the front, only the ends of the bar will protrude beyond the circle. Before gluing the bar to the circle, sand and buff ½" (1 cm) on each end of the bar. After buffing, gild each end with gold wax, and buff with a soft cloth. Caution: Do not use the wax on the center portion of the pin bar; if you do, the glue will not adhere to it (Photo 3, left, shows gilded pin bar).

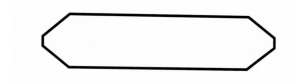

Pattern for pin bar.

3. The dangle is attached to the center piece. At left, pin bar and Art Deco face.

Faces for brooches.

5. Graphic Transfer (Face)

a. For the picture portion of this piece, roll out the ecru clay on the #3 setting (3/32", 2.4 mm) of the pasta machine. Cut an ecru oval or rectangle to fit in the circle, and then choose which graphic you wish to use from the samples, or pick your own graphic.

b. Photocopy and cut out the Art Deco face or other graphic that you want to use, and color it with colored pencils. Refer to the Black-and-White Transfers section of the book for making the transfer. Bake the ecru piece and cool.

c. Sand around the edges of the baked piece, being careful not to sand any of the transfer portion. Gild the edges with gold wax. Center the picture piece on the black circle and glue on with cyanoacrylate glue.

6. Finishing:
Connect the circle piece to the hanging faux Bakelite piece using two large jump rings (Photo 3). Glue the pin bar onto the back of the circle so that the gilded tips show on each side. Glue the pin back to the pin bar. If you wish to wear your pin as a pendant, cut a piece of clear plastic tubing that is the width of your pin. Thread a cord through the tubing (Photo 4) and put necklace fasteners on the ends of the cord. Open the pin back and slip the tube onto the sharp bar of the pin and close the pin. You now have a pendant to wear.

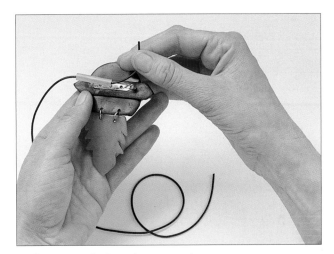

4. Converting the brooch to a pendant.

MINIATURE BOWLS

Designer
Dotty McMillan (inspired by Carolyn Potter)

*W*hat fun it is to make realistic things much smaller than they normally are! These bowls are no exception. They are fun and fast and let your imagination soar. Make them one solid color or use a cane slice as a base, trim with tiny cane slices, use mokume gane slices, or antique them. These can go into a dollhouse or on a shelf — or string them on a cord to wear.

MATERIALS

Polymer clay:

    Colors of your choice, total 1 oz or less (28 g)

    Small amount of waste clay

    Canes for making and decorating bowls*

    Scrap clay for decorations

See Making Canes section of book.

Glass marbles**

Sharp blade

Pasta machine

Round cookie cutter, about 1" (2.5 cm) in diameter, or something else to cut circles

Cornstarch

**One or more in the sizes you want for your bowls. You can also make a clay marble the size you want, sanding and buffing it so that it's very smooth.*

1. Make a small pad of waste clay and press the marble into it, going no more than one-third of the way down the depth of the pad with the marble. Remove the marble and bake the pad. You will use this to rest the marble in whenever you make a tiny bowl. It will keep the marble from rolling around in the oven while baking.

2. Roll out some clay on the second- or third-thickest setting of the pasta machine (⁷⁄₆₄" or ³⁄₃₂", 2.8 or 2.4 mm). Cut out a circle from clay that is approximately 1" (2.5 cm) in diameter, depending on the size of your marble, or cut a cane slice of 1" in diameter instead. It should fit halfway down the marble after it is applied. Putting a dab of cornstarch on the clay before molding it to the marble is helpful to keep it from sticking.

3. Gently mold your clay circle or cane slice around and down the sides of the marble (photo). Do not go below the middle of the marble. If you do, it will be difficult to remove the clay from the marble after it is baked. Your bowl is upside down at this point. Decide on what type of base or foot you want your bowl to have. Flatten a small ball of clay or use a cane slice for a foot for the bowl. Firmly press the foot onto the bottom of the bowl.

4. Make as many other bowls as you like. Bake each with the marble in place; while it is still warm, carefully remove the bowl from the marble.

5. Decorate your bowls any way you like: add tiny cane slices, small snakes of clay, handles, etc. Bake the bowls again, this time upright, sitting on their feet. For a shiny glass or porcelain look, give the pieces three or four coats of a clay-compatible glaze.

A cane slice is placed over the marble, to shape a bowl.

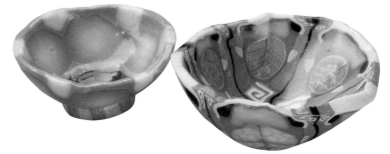

TINY JOINTED TEDDY BEAR

Designer
Kathy Davis

Kathy is a wonderful dollmaker whose creations depict delightfully free-spirited images. See the Gallery section of the book for more of Kathy's work. Her tiny jointed teddies are favorites of many collectors. They will no doubt become a favorite of yours also. Says Kathy: "This is an easy and fun project. It is small enough that it doesn't take very long to complete and it's perfect for using up little bits of leftover clay."

MATERIALS

Polymer clay: Various brands and colors (see Kathy's note below)

    For bear: 2 oz (56 g) of color you choose

    For eyes: small amount of black

Sculpting tool

Small piece of mat board or cardboard

Large round-ended tapestry needle

3 long doll needles or long hatpins

3-inch (7.5 cm) flathead pin

20-gauge craft wire, about 2 feet (61 cm)

Round-nose pliers

Chain-nose pliers

Scissors

Flush cutters, wire trimmer, or sturdy fingernail cutters

Black gesso or acrylic paint

Acrylic wood stain

Bits of lace

Glue or needle and thread

Kathy notes: "I normally use mixtures of clay. My favorite mixture is a combination of Super Sculpey and Cernit. I mix them in proportions of anywhere between 50/50 to 75/25 (Super Sculpey to Cernit). I also mix flesh-colored clays and add small bits of colored clay to tint the clay. I like the natural look the clay has from adding the colored clay to the flesh tones. That way the colors aren't too saturated. To get a good brown tone, I often find it necessary to balance browns with a bit of bright green, otherwise they end up being too red. Using a color wheel, you can easily learn to balance colors. By experimenting with small bits of clay, you'll soon discover colors that you'll enjoy using. Remember, all bears don't have to be brown or tan. Have fun and experiment."

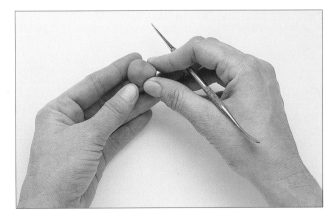

1. Carefully shape the head.

1. Eyes. You can make your own teddy bear eyes out of black clay. Form them in the shape of cloves so that they can be set well into the teddy's head. Small beads could be used instead, but if there is no clay around them to trap them, they could fall out later. Bake your clay eyes for about 10 minutes on a small piece of mat board.

2. Sculpting the Head

a. Start with a small ball of clay, about ¾" (2 cm) across. Pull the lower part of the face forward to form the muzzle (Photo 1). At the neck, the point where the head meets the body, make a slight indentation to fit the body curve. To form the nose, first mark the top edge with a straight sculpting tool. Then follow around the outside edge of the snout to define the nose as desired. It can be oval, triangular, or realistic, with nostrils defined, as you prefer.

b. Mark the mouth with three simple lines, the first straight down from the nose and then two marks extended slightly down and out to form the mouth (see finished bear). The ends can curve upwards into a smile. This way you can control the bear's expression.

c. Push the prebaked eyes into the head where you think they look good. Note how the eye placement also affects the bear's expression. You can add eyelids if you wish, using tiny "worms" of clay.

d. To form the ears, take a tiny piece of clay and form it into a ball. Flatten the ball, keeping the edges a bit thicker than the center. With a small pair of scissors, clip the flattened piece in half to form the two ears. Attach the ears in the desired positions. Make sure they are connected securely to the head all around the ear.

e. Now that the head is sculpted, you can mark the fur on your bear's head. Use a large tapestry needle with a round tip. You can either mark the fur over the entire head or leave the muzzle bare. Leave the inside of the ears bare.

3. Sculpting the Body

a. The bear's body (torso) is about 1½ times as long as the head. (The arms and legs are made separately from the body.) Take a piece of clay larger than the head and form it into the shape of a kidney bean, with the tummy curving outwards and the back curving inwards. The top or neck area should be narrower than the bottom. With your fingers, gently press in to form round spots (depressions) where the arms and legs will connect. Check the fit of the head and body, and adjust if needed. When the body is shaped to your satisfaction, mark the fur in a downward direction.

b. Use a small piece of clay to form the arm. It can be about the same length as the body. The top of the arm should be flat and round on the side facing the body; the paws can curve gently inward. Make a second arm in mirror image to the first to make sure you have a right and left arm. Mark the paw pad if desired. The leg requires a bit more clay than the arm. It should be flat and round at the inner hip, where it will attach to the body. The bottom of the leg widens gently into a paw. You can mark the foot pad if you wish. Some actual teddy bears have stitches for claws. Experiment and see if marks in the clay look good to you. Mark the fur on the arms and legs.

4. Jointing

a. Now you are ready to make the holes for the jointing. Starting with the head, insert a long doll needle into the center of the bottom of the head, and upward through the top of the head, between the ears. Gently twist the needle to ease it into place. After it has gone through successfully, take the needle out and reinsert it in the opposite direction through the same hole. This makes a nice clean hole.

b. Take the needle and insert it into the body from the top (center of the neck) to the bottom. The more you get used to inserting the needle through the body parts, the easier it gets. Remove the needle and reinsert it in the opposite direction as you did for the head. This time, place the head on top of the body with the needle in place to check the fit.

c. Take a second doll needle and insert it through the center of the round depression in the body where the arm will attach, and aim for the center of the depression on the body for the opposite arm. You don't want to hit the needle holding the head, however. It helps to have the head needle in place, as the second needle normally will slide past. Reverse the needle to clear the hole.

d. Put the arm next to the body where you want it to attach. The same wire will go through the body at the shoulders to hold on the arms, so take each arm and make a hole with the doll needle at the center point of the outer shoulder, going through the body and out through the opposite arm's shoulder. Reverse the arm needle and clear the hole.

e. With the doll needle, pierce through the body at the hips, in the same way you did for the arms (Photo 2). Place the leg next to the body at the hip, where you want it to attach, and pierce the leg with the needle at the hip, in the same way you did for the arm. Repeat for second leg. Assemble the bear on 3 long needles or pins and check the whole bear's fit.

f. Remove the needles and bake your bear at the clay manufacturer's recommended temperature for 30 minutes.

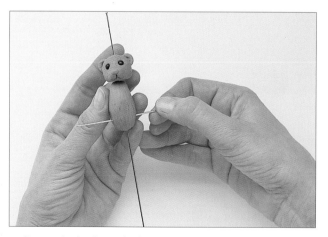

2. Pierce the body at the hips with a needle.

5. Assembling. To assemble your bear, take a 3-inch head pin and insert it from the bottom of the bear's body upwards, adding the head on top of the body. Form a loop on top of the bear's head with the end of the pin; cut off any excess (Photo 3). For the arms, take

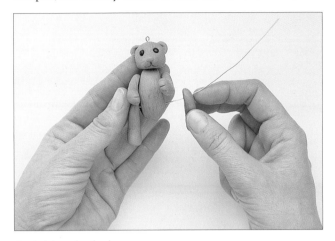

3. Adding the final piece.

a piece of 20-gauge craft wire and form a small circle on one end with round-nose pliers. Bend the circle perpendicular to the rest of the wire with the pliers, so it will lie flat along the arm. This forms the end to hold the arm in place. Place the arm on the wire, put the wire through the arm hole in the body, and add the other arm on the other side of the body. Make sure both arms are on correctly before making another flat loop at the other end of the wire to hold them on. Trim off excess wire. Repeat this process for the legs (Photo 3).

6. Finishing. To finish your bear, paint the nose with black gesso or acrylic paint. When the nose is completely dry, stain the entire bear with an acrylic wood stain. The stain gives a nice depth to the fur and a lovely finish to the bear. Sew or glue on a ruff of lace at the bear's neck for a nice finishing touch to your bear. Have fun making bears! This basic idea can be converted to make many types of animals. Antiqued and collared, Teddy makes a great present.

SPIFFY LITTLE LADIES

Designer
Dotty McMillan

Here is a good way to use up left-over canes and create an elegant brooch that looks wonderful on the lapel of a suit or the side of a sweater. For those who feel face-cane impaired, don't worry. These little ladies don't require a cane slice for their features. Their pretty faces are from a pen-and-ink drawing, which is put onto the clay as a simple black-and-white photo transfer.

MATERIALS

Polymer clay:

    Flesh or beige-toned clay, any brand, 1 oz (28 g)

    Black clay, 1 oz (28 g)

    A variety of canes*

    Scraps of other colors for clothes

    Translucent Liquid Sculpey

Pasta machine or acrylic roller

*See Making Canes section of book if you need canes.

Sharp blade

Small, sharp scissors

Waxed paper or bakery tissue

Wet/dry sandpaper in 320, 400, and 600 grits

Buffing equipment

Acrylic paints (optional)

Pin back

Cyanoacrylate glue such as Zap-a-Gap

1. The Image. Photocopy a face included here, or find or draw your own line drawing of a face and photocopy it. Enlarge or reduce if necessary to the right size for the brooch you want. If you have a computer and laser printer (not an inkjet), you can scan in any one of these and print it yourself. Cut out the image from the paper.

Faces for your transfers.

2. Transferring Face Image to Clay. Roll out the flesh-toned or beige clay on the #3 setting (3/32", 2.4 mm) of the pasta machine. Place the clay on whatever surface you will use for baking. Lay the photocopy face down on the surface of the clay. Trim around it with the sharp blade. Burnish the surface carefully, making certain that all of the paper is well seated on the clay. Do not lift the clay at this point as it will almost always lift the paper. Place the baking surface and clay into a preheated oven (heated to the recommended temperature for the clay) and bake for five minutes. Remove from the oven and carefully peel off the paper; replace the clay in the oven and complete the baking time. Let the piece cool. Use a bit of dry rouge or blusher to tint the lady's cheeks. Trim around the piece with small, sharp scissors and set aside.

3. Black Backing. Roll out a sheet of black clay on the #3 setting (3/32" or 2.4 mm) of the pasta machine. Make certain the sheet will be large enough to fit the entire area of the baked piece, which it will back. Coat the back of the baked face with a thin layer of Translucent Liquid Sculpey and place it in the center of the black sheet of clay.

4. Wardrobe

a. Decide what colors and cane patterns you wish to use for your lady's wardrobe. You might do a sketch to determine which pieces should be laid down first, and which can be laid on top of other pieces. There is no end to what your imagination can conjure for these outfits. They can be subtle and sedate or wild and outlandish. Just about anything goes. If your canes are old, recondition them by warming them in your hands; then press down on the top of them, roll or squeeze out a bit, press down again, and repeat over and over until you can feel them moving well, inside and out.

1. After the baked transfer face is laid onto a back of raw black clay, "clothing" is planned.

b. Place your baked clay face with black clay backing on the baking surface so that it will not have to be moved when it's ready to be baked. Begin to "dress" your lovely lady with clay scraps by cutting and arranging slices from canes and solid clay pieces (Photo 1). Once you are pleased with the results, use a sharp blade, craft knife, or needle tool to trim off the excess black clay around the outside edge of the lady (Photo 2). Use your fingers and blade to smooth around the

2. Trim away the excess black clay.

edges and gently press the black and front piece together. Place the entire piece in the oven and bake for the recommended length of time. Let cool.

5. Sanding. Caution: Do not sand the face portion of the piece as that will remove the graphic transfer. Wet-sand the back and front of your lady, starting with the 320 grit and working up to the 600. Don't sand the surface so hard that you remove any of the small details. Concentrate on the rougher areas. Sand around the edges of the piece. Buff the piece with a buffing wheel, or by hand with a soft cotton towel. The wheel will give the piece a nice shine, while the towel will give it a soft sheen.

6. Finishing. Glue on a pin back. If you are good with painting small details, you might want to tint the lady's lips with rose or red acrylic paint and touch the eyes with a bit of blue and a tiny dab of white.

It's fun to have a collection of these brooches that reflect your moods or the seasons. For winter you can wrap your lady in a snug textured collar (use a heavy-grit #32 sandpaper for texture) and a fur-like hat (imitation clay fur, of course). In spring, small pastel patterns are nice, with a large flowery hat. Summer brings on bright colors and tiny hats, or no hats, using instead an upswept hairdo trimmed with colorful clips. Fall is a good time for rust and gold and copper colors.

SPIRAL CHOKER

Designer
Cheryl Trottier

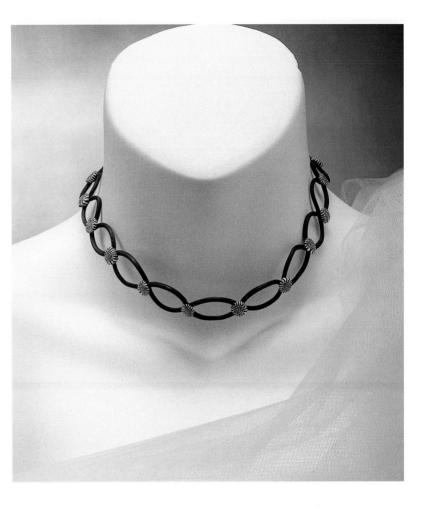

heryl is a talented Canadian polymer clay artist. Her delicate spiral rope necklace is very lightweight and easy to make. It is the small, delicate type of design that appeals to many teen-agers as well as adults.

MATERIALS

Polymer clay:

  Sculpey SuperFlex clay in your choice of colors, ½ oz (14 g); the sample project shown used black

  A cane of your choice, about 1/4" (0.6 cm) in diameter × 1" (2.5 cm) long*

Graph paper

Pencil

Kemper™ clay gun

Parchment paper or tracing paper (see-through surface that can be heated)

Sharp blade

*See Making Canes section of book.

1. Draw a line of ovals, each of which is ¾" long × ½" wide (2 × 1.2 cm) on graph paper. You will need 13 to 15 ovals, depending on the length you wish the finished piece to be, which is probably about 14" to 16" (35 to 40 cm).

2. SuperFlex clay sometimes starts out very hard. If so, use the following method to condition it. Place the clay in a small plastic bag and then immerse in hot tap water (not boiling water, as this would quickly bake the clay). This will soften it and make the clay workable. Also place your clay gun in a plastic bag in hot water or set it under a desk lamp to warm.

3. Set the clay gun to the second- or third-smallest hole, about 2 mm. Place the warmed clay inside the warmed clay gun. Extrude a "snake" 20" to 22" long (50 to 55 cm); see Photo 1. Leave the snake under a

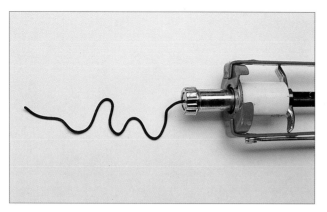

1. Extrude a long "snake" of flexible clay.

5. Extrude a second clay snake just like the first one. Lay this snake over the top of the straight 1-inch end of the first snake, and then follow the pattern curves in the opposite direction from the curves of the first snake, ending up with a straight piece over the 2" (5 cm) straight piece on the first snake.

6. Take the 1" long (2.5 cm) straight ends and twist them together to make a spiral rope. Curve this piece into a loop. Take the 2" (5 cm) ends and twist them together into a spiral rope, but leave this end unbent. Make 3 balls of clay each ⅛" (3 mm) in diameter, and press them firmly into the straight spiral rope piece, placing the balls about ⅜" (10 mm) apart to make your choker adjustable. The balls will go through the loop to close the choker.

desk lamp to keep it from becoming hard again too soon. It will not stick to itself if it is cold.

4. Place parchment paper or other see-through surface or a sheet of glass over your oval pattern. Lay the length of the clay snake in a series of wave curves (Photo 2), following the pattern, leaving 1" (2.5 cm) straight extra at one end and 2" (5 cm) at the other.

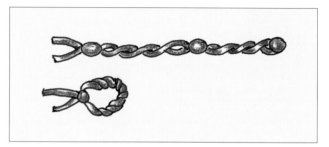

Ends of choker: Twist short end and shape into a loop. Twist the other end and add knobs of clay for closure.

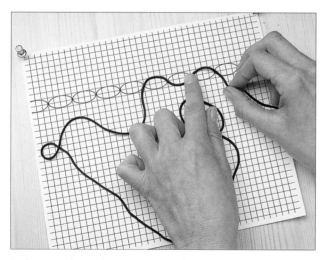

2. Lay out the snake according to the pattern.

7. Slice as many pieces from your pattern cane as you have curves. Firmly press one slice into the joins of the curves (overlaps). Bake the piece on parchment paper for the manufacturer's recommended time and temperature. Let cool.

Designer's note: SuperFlex clay is a special polymer clay that remains flexible after it is baked. However, I have found that it can become brittle if it has a second baking.

DESIGNER BUTTONS

Designer
Dotty McMillan

Here is the perfect project for anyone who sews. Make your own designer buttons, or give them as presents. Top that off by making earrings to match. Buttons can be made in any size, from a hefty coat button to a dainty blouse button. The secret to the look of these particular buttons is that they use a kaleidoscope type of cane. There are many techniques for making kaleidoscope canes; this is just one of them. Others can be found in clay books, videos, and magazine articles. These buttons are washable, unless they have been glazed.

MATERIALS

Polymer clay:

Colors you want, 2 oz (28 g) of each color, about 6 oz (84 g) in total

Flower cane or other large pattern cane (optional)*

Colored pencils and drawing paper (or a computer paint program)

Ruler

Sharp blade

See Making Canes section of book.

Set of circle cutters (optional)

Needle tool or rubber stamps

Wet/dry sandpaper in 320, 400, and 600 grits

Burnt sienna acrylic paint for antiquing (optional)

Soft cotton towel or a buffing wheel

Button shanks and earring posts

Cyanoacrylate glue

1. Designing the Cane

a. If you haven't made a cane yet, see the Making Canes section of the book before starting. Your first step is to design a triangular kaleidoscope cane on paper. This may sound difficult, but is actually easy. Using your ruler or a template, draw a triangle with all three sides equal in length (equilateral triangle). Each angle of such a triangle is 60 degrees, and when 6 of the triangles are put with the points together, you will have a full 360 degrees of a circle for your button top, in the same way a kaleidoscope makes a full circle out of repeating triangle images. Make the triangle about 2½" (6.5 cm) on each side. Using your colored pencils or crayons, begin filling in the inside areas of the triangle with different shapes.

b. If you have a flower cane or other large pattern cane you want to use in your design, sketch it in your drawing about two-thirds of the way from the top point. Add a triangle of color at the top point. Add colored triangles alongside the flower cane. If you do not have an already made flower cane, then plan a simple bull's-eye or jelly roll cane using three colors. Draw this into your pattern. Fill in the rest of the triangle with small triangles, checkerboards, squares, circles, etc.

c. Make sure you have covered the whole triangle with designs. Take two small mirrors and hold them on the right and left side lines of the triangle. You can now see how the repeated pattern will look. Or photocopy or trace the triangle 5 more times on a copier and paste the design parts together and color them to preview the whole pattern. (If you have access to a computer paint drawing program, you can draw a triangle and copy and join the triangles to see the same thing.) This is only a cursory glimpse of your design, however, as it will appear somewhat different after it is reduced in size. You can determine if you like the color choices and how they look together, as well as how the lines of the design will run when all six triangular pieces of the kaleidoscope cane are together with the points meeting in the center.

2. Making the Cane

a. Once you are satisfied with your design, begin making your triangle cane out of clay. It will be a triangular solid or prism shape. The cross-section of the cane should be the same size as your triangle drawing. Start with the bottom level (base of triangle) and work upward, adding the various colors, sizes, and shapes of clay as you go. (See the section of the book on Making Canes for reference.) Make sure you keep the triangle shape and keep the sides of equal length (Photo 1).

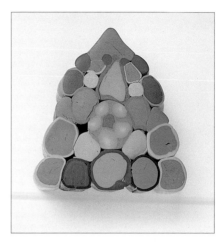

1. Canes and logs are stacked to form a triangular cane.

b. When your triangular cane is built, you may choose to leave it unwrapped, or you may wrap it with a thin sheet (#5 on the pasta machine, ¹⁄₁₆" or 1.6 mm) of black, white, or another color of clay that will stand out in the finished piece. Black and white are usually safe choices, but don't be afraid to experiment. If you wrap only the right and left side of the triangle and not the bottom, you will get a different effect than if you wrap all three sides. If you wrap just the bottom side with a different color, you will get another effect. Designing these canes is where the fun comes in.

3. Reducing the Cane. Reducing a triangular cane is a bit more difficult than reducing a round or square cane. Start by setting the triangular cane on end and use the palms and heels of your hands to press in on two sides; then turn the cane and press in on two sides again, continuing on around several turns. Then flip the cane over and bring the other end up and do the same. After the cane is easier to handle, lay it lengthwise on the worktable in front of you and begin pinching in on the top edge of the triangle and at the same time pressing it downward and pulling outward. Pinch, press, and then tug outward. Turn the piece one turn and repeat. Pick the piece up now and then and give it a small stretch; then continue with the pinching, pressing, and tugging. Reduce and extrude the cane until it is 6" (15 cm) long after the mucky ends have been removed.

4. Assembling the Triangles. Lay the cane on one of its 6" (15 cm) sides and cut the cane into three 2" long (5 cm) pieces (Photo 2). Measure carefully so that they are all equal. Fit the three pieces together so that the parts of the design on each piece that were at the top of the triangle in your drawing meet at the center (Photo 3). Once the three pieces are fitted together, flip the resulting cane on its side, measure and mark the center, and cut its length in half. Join the two halves together, still keeping tops of the triangle designs meeting at the center. If there is a gap in the center, add a tiny log of color or a small jelly roll cane (Photo 4). Press all the pieces together snugly to avoid any gaps. Use any method of reducing the cane to the size you want for your buttons. (See reducing canes in the Making Canes section of book).

5. Making the Buttons

a. Your reduced cane will be round. Slice off equally thick pieces of the cane for your buttons. Using a compatible color of clay, roll out a sheet on the #4 setting (5/64" or 2 mm) of the pasta machine. For each slice, cut out a backing piece that is about ¼" (0.6 cm) larger in diameter than your cane slice. You can use a set of circle cutters for this if you adapt your cane slice diameter to fit. Set your cane slice in the middle of the backing clay circle.

b. Roll out a snake in either the same color as the backing or in black. This will be used to frame your buttons. The diameter of the snake for framing should be very small. A little experimenting will give you the right size. Wrap this snake around the outside of each of the cane slices on top of the portion of the backing that shows around the edge. Impress the snake with a needle tool, a small rubber stamp, or any other item that will make a small impression (Photo 5).

c. Bake and cool your buttons.

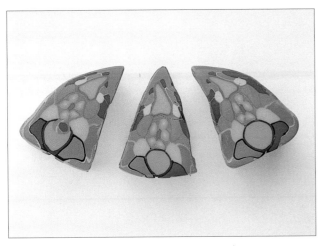

2. From the reduced triangle cane, three equal pieces are cut.

4. The assembled halves make a circular cane of 6 triangles.

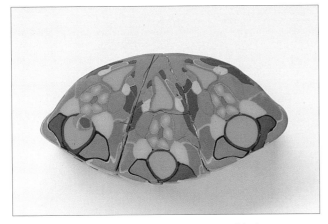

3. The three pieces of triangle cane are assembled.

6. Sanding and Buffing. Lightly sand all sides of the buttons. Start with the 320 grit wet/dry sandpaper, go to the 400, and then use the 600, always sanding with water. You can go to a finer sandpaper if you prefer the finish it gives. Buff the surface of the front side of the buttons with a soft cotton towel. This will give them a lovely sheen. If you wish to have a glasslike shine, buff on a buffing wheel.

7. Antiquing (Optional). You may like the effect of antiquing on some of your buttons. Do this after you have completed Step 6. Use a rather stiff brush and a small amount of burnt sienna acrylic paint. With a dabbing motion, add paint all over the front portion of the button. The dabbing motion helps to get the paint into the recessed areas of the texturing on the rim of the button. Wipe off the excess paint and continue wiping until you are satisfied with the results. You can remove all of the paint from the pattern area and leave it in just the outside rim, if you wish. Wipe all of the paint off the back of the button.

8. Gluing on Shanks. Glue a button shank on the back with some cyanoacrylate glue. You can make some lovely earrings with these button shapes by gluing on earring posts instead of button shanks.

There are many other ways to make buttons with polymer clay. It would take an entire book to cover them all. Once you have made these buttons, go on to develop other methods. A wonderful book to give you a look at a wide variety of buttons is *The Book of Buttons* by Joyce Whittemore.

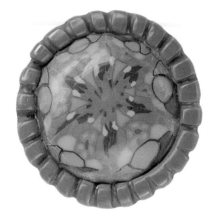

5. Button with decorative edge that has been antiqued.

THUMB RINGS

Designer
Dotty McMillan

Thumb rings are in fashion. Most of the ones you see are made of sterling silver, but why not make them with polymer clay? You can make them in whatever colors, patterns, and styles you want. If they are baked correctly, thumb rings wear just fine and are very comfortable. These rings are so easy and fun that I bet you can't make just one. Of course, rings don't have to be limited to thumb rings. You can go on from here and design ones for just about any finger on your hand. Just don't make them too thick and bulky, as that will cause them to be uncomfortable.

MATERIALS

Polymer clay:

Inside of ring base color: Any kind of clay except Sculpey, which isn't strong enough. Black, deep brown, gray, silver, and gold are all good colors to consider; about 1 oz (28 g)

Pattern cane slices: Use new canes or old leftover ones, or bits and pieces of brightly colored canes, or black-and-white geometric cane slices

Sharp blade: a wavy blade is a good second choice for an interesting edge

Talcum powder or cornstarch

Ring mandrel (optional, but a great help) or a dowel with the same circumference as the thumb you are trying to fit. Or (less accurate, but possible), your thumb

Acrylic roller or brayer

Waxed paper

1. Roll out your base clay on the #1 setting (⅛", 3.2 mm) of the pasta machine. Cut a strip of clay about 3" long x 2" wide (7.5 × 5 cm) and lay it on a piece of waxed paper. Take very thin (1 to 2 mm) slices from the canes and cover the base clay strip with them (Photo 1). Place a piece of waxed paper over the top and, using your roller or brayer, roll the slices into the base clay. It doesn't hurt if some of the slices are slightly raised; it all depends on the look you want.

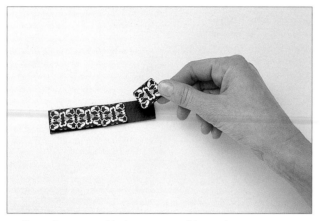

1. Cane slices are added to a strip of base clay.

2. Use your blade to cut the strip of clay to a width of ½" to ¾" (1 to 2 cm), depending on how wide a ring is comfortable for you to wear. The length will depend on the size of the ring. If you have a ring mandrel, wrap the clay around it at the ring size you need (Photo 2), and overlap the clay end. On the inside of the ring, lightly mark where the circumference of your finger ends and the clay starts to overlap. Remove the clay from the mandrel and cut the strip about ¼" (0.6 cm) beyond the mark you made. This ¼" will be the overlap that holds the ring together. Coat the base clay

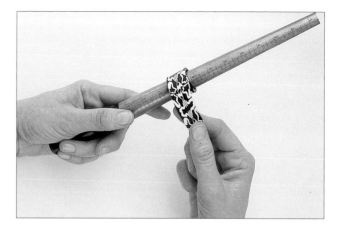

2. The ring is shaped and sized on a ring mandrel. Leave an overlap for joining.

interior of ring with talc or cornstarch, but do not cover the ¼" of the overlap or it will not stick to the other end of the ring. Follow the same procedure if you are using a dowel or your thumb to measure.

3. Rewrap the clay around the mandrel, dowel, or your thumb, overlap the ¼" of clay, and press the top layer end together with the other end of the ring. Slip it off the mandrel, dowel, or your thumb and press again on the overlap, but not too hard, or you will expand the size of the ring. Adjust the ring so that it is round, and slip it on your thumb to make sure it will go over the knuckle. Bake and let cool.

Your ring should fit so that it slips snugly over the wide part of your thumb and rests on the narrower part between the first and second joint. If it should turn out too large, you can easily make it smaller by adding a very thin sheet of clay inside the ring. I emphasize "thin" because it takes very little to decrease the size. You can always add more, but you can't make the ring any larger once it is baked.

DARK CRYSTAL JEWELRY

Designer
Dotty McMillan

*I*t's not difficult to create a stunning articulated brooch and matching earrings encrusted with dark crystal mokume gane. This luscious jewelry looks as if it were made for a medieval queen. The brooch is easily converted into a pendant whenever you wish a change (see Art Deco Brooch for this process). Using colored translucents, metallic foils, rubber stamps, metallic wax, and muslin or silk cloth, create these unique pieces; you will then find yourself overflowing with more creative ideas.

1. Preparing the Clays. Tint about 2 ounces of the translucent Premo! clay with a small amount of the alizarin crimson; use just enough color to achieve a rich, deep pink. Mix well. Add a small bit of orange clay to another 2 ounces of translucent Premo! to get a nice warm orange. Mix well. Follow the instructions for making an impressed from top mokume gane pad in the Techniques section of the book, using the tinted translucent clays. Alternate layers — pink clay, a sheet of foil, a sheet of orange clay — and then repeat until the pad is about 1 to 1½" (2.5 to 3.5 cm) thick. If you

wish, make your top sheet of clay an opaque black one. Do the impressing by pushing down with your texturing tools from the top of the clay pad. Begin slicing off very thin slices of the mokume pad, and place them on a sheet of waxed paper.

2. Making the Mokume Gane Hearts

a. Roll out a sheet of translucent clay on the #3 setting (³⁄₃₂", 2.4 mm) of the pasta machine. Lay slices of your mokume gane onto the translucent sheet, overlapping them just slightly. Place the clay between two pieces of waxed paper, and roll over it

MATERIALS

Polymer clay:

    Bleached Translucent Premo! Sculpey, 3 oz (84 g)

    Black clay, 1 oz (28 g), optional

    Small amount of alizarin crimson and orange clays for tinting

    Translucent Liquid Sculpey

Gold or silver wax (available at most craft stores)

Gold, silver, or copper foil — at least 5 sheets

Various impressing tools: Phillips head screwdriver, thick-toothed comb, etc.

¼ yard (25 cm) unbleached muslin or printed cotton which has been washed, or pure silk

Cyanoacrylate glue

Waxed paper

Acrylic roller

Pasta machine

Ruler

Sharp blade

2" wide (5 cm) and 1½" wide (4 cm) heart-shaped cookie cutters (optional)

Scissors

Wet/dry sandpaper in 320, 400, and 600 grits

Sponge and small bowl

Buffing equipment

Pin and earring findings

with an acrylic roller or brayer. Turn the strip over and roll some more. When the piece is as smooth as you can get it without stretching it out too much, remove the waxed paper. For the brooch, cut out a 2" (5 cm) wide heart-shaped piece from the clay with a cutter or blade. Cut out 1½" (3.8 cm) wide heart-shaped pieces for the earrings. Place the pieces on your baking surface.

b. Cut each heart-shaped piece of clay into horizontal segments about ¼" (0.6 cm) wide. Some segments may be slightly wider or narrower. This doesn't matter,

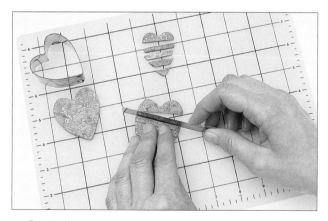

1. Cut the heart into sections.

unless you are determined that they all be absolutely equal. I rather like things that are not totally even or symmetrical. Do not move the segments; leave them exactly as they are when you cut them.

c. Overbake the clay by raising the temperature to 300°F (149°C) during the last five minutes of baking, and let cool. When cool, break the segments apart (they tend to stick somewhat), but again, do not change their positions.

3. Attaching the Cloth. For each heart, lay out your cotton or silk material on your work surface and cut a piece of it that is about ¼" (0.6 cm) larger around than your clay heart. Place it on a piece of paper. Brush a coating of Translucent Liquid Sculpey onto the cloth. Be sure you don't miss any area of the cloth. Carefully lay each segment of the heart onto the cloth in the same position that it had before. The backs of the segments touch the cloth. Lift the paper, put the pieces into the oven, and bake.

4. Separating the Segments. Check each segment and make certain the cloth is well adhered to the baked clay, especially at the corners. If any spot is loose, secure it with a tiny dab of cyanoacrylate glue. Trim the excess material around the edges of each heart with a pair of small, sharp scissors (Photo 2). When the pieces are cool, carefully snap the segments so that they are loose. Sometimes this takes a bit of encouragement with your blade. The segments are now all held together by the cloth backing, but the piece is wonderfully flexible (Photo 3).

5. Sanding and Finishing. Sand the mokume surface of the brooch and earrings starting with a 320 grit wet/dry paper, then a 400 grit, and finish with a 600.

Do not submerge the pieces in water! Use a bowl of water and carefully sponge off the surface you are sanding without wetting the cloth backing. Buff the surface with either a buffing wheel, a Dremel tool with a cotton wheel, or a soft cotton towel. Add a pin back and your brooch is ready to wear.

This technique can be used to make many other wonderful items. Set your brain to thinking about what they might be.

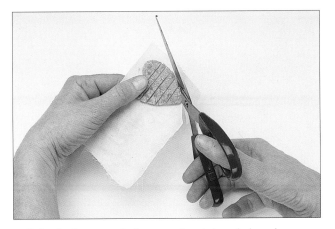

2. Bake the heart on cloth covered with liquid clay; then cut the heart out of the fabric.

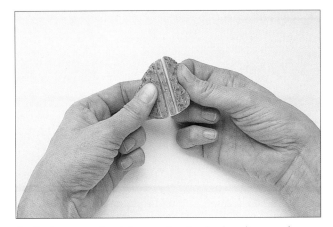

3. Segments are freed from each other by bending, so the piece moves well.

COLLAGE PIN

Designer
Dotty McMillan,
inspired by polymer clay artist
Mari O'Dell.

This is a fun project which will stir up all sorts of design ideas. The technique consists of taking readymade designs, cutting them into segments, and then reassembling them into a design that is all your own. Using this technique you can create all the wild fantasy images your imagination can come up with.

MATERIALS

Polymer clay (any brand): white, 2 oz (56 g)	Rubber cement or white glue
Copy shop or laser print-outs of a variety of graphic images	Cyanoacrylate glue
Colored pencils	Brown acrylic paint for antiquing frame
Craft knife or blade	Wet/dry sandpaper in 400 and 600 grit
Needle tool	Scissors
Texturing tool	Pin back

1. Creating Your Image

a. Start by cutting up your graphic images and laying them all out in front of you (Photo 1). Begin arranging and rearranging the pieces until you get an image that pleases you. For instance, cut out a head from one graphic, a hat from another, a torso from another, and some clothing from another. Reassemble them into an entirely new image. Make certain that your reassembled image is the size you wish for the center of your pin (or you can have a copy of it reduced at a copy shop). Remember that you will be adding a frame, which will increase the overall size of your pin. Once you are pleased with your image, lay it on a piece of white paper and attach it with rubber cement or glue. Photocopy this image and keep the glued one as your master so you can use the image again.

1. Make a collage using a variety of images.

b. Using colored pencils, color the new photocopy of your image (Photo 2). Don't forget to color the background. Don't skimp on the coloring. Make certain it is applied fairly heavily. Don't worry if your coloring isn't perfect. By the time you are finished, slight mistakes won't show. Cut out your image, leaving at least ¼" (0.6 cm) of white paper around the decorated portion.

2. Transfer the Image. Condition your white clay well. Roll out a sheet on the thickest setting of your pasta machine (⅛", 3.2 mm). Cut out a square, rectangle, circle, or an oval, whichever fits best with the size and shape of your image. Place the clay piece onto

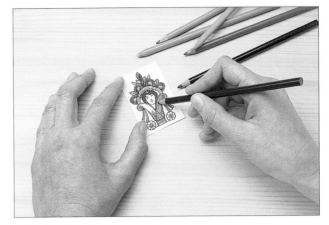

2. Color the photocopy.

whatever surface you will use for baking it. Follow the directions in the Black-and-White Transfers with Colored Pencils section of the book to do the transfer, including baking.

3. The Frame. Once your transfer is done and your image piece is baked for the full length of time, trim the edges slightly with a sharp pair of scissors. Sand the edges lightly to smooth. Condition and then roll out a sheet of white clay on the #3 setting (³₃₂", 2.4 mm) of the pasta machine. Place the clay with the transfer in the center of the sheet of white clay and trim around it so that you have about ¼" (0.6 cm) of the white showing around the edges. Roll out a snake of white clay ¼" (0.6 cm) wide and long enough to fit completely around the edge of the white clay that extends beyond the photo transfer piece as a frame. Fit the snake to the piece and press slightly to make sure it is adhered. Using a texture tool, impress and mark the frame around the entire piece. Bake the piece.

4. Final Steps

Once your piece has cooled, check to make sure that the clay with the transfer is firmly in place in the frame. Try snapping it out. If it won't come out, that's fine. If it does come out, put a few dabs of cyanoacrylate glue on the back and fit it back into place. Sand and buff all but the transfer area, and antique the whole frame. Glue the pin back on the back.

Note: There are many variations. You could gild the whole piece or emphasize parts of the image with gel pens, for example.

MUSIC PIN

Designer
Dotty McMillan

This is a quick and easy method of creating special interest jewelry. People are always looking for items that reflect their hobbies, careers, sports, or pets. Some people collect things that represent frogs, sunflowers, dragonflies, hummingbirds, cats, dogs, wild animals, children, etc. The same simple technique used for the music pin shown here can be applied to just about any interest.

MATERIALS

Polymer clay:

    White, 1 oz (28 g)

    Black, 1 oz (28 g)

    Small amount of Translucent Liquid Sculpey

Black-and-white graphics (e.g., piano shape with musical instruments, notes, etc.)

Scissors

Sharp blade or Exacto knife

Pasta machine

Wet/dry sandpaper in 320, 400, and 600 grits

Small white seed beads

Pin back

Cyanoacrylate glue

1. Choose a black-and-white music graphic or use the one with this project. (Books and the Internet are good sources of graphics.) Once you have your graphic, get it reduced or enlarged to the size you want at a copy shop. Note that a transfer will end up reversed on the clay. The one here is already reversed so when you put it on the clay it will end up unreversed. If you have a computer and a laser printer, you can size it and print it yourself. See the Black-and-White Transfers section of the book for details. Cut around the piano image, leaving a small white margin.

Transfer pattern for music pin (reversed).

Larger version of notes (reversed).

2. Roll out the white clay on the #1 setting (⅛", 3.2 mm) of the pasta machine. Cut a piece of white clay that is larger than the piano shape. You will cut it to the piano shape after baking. Place the clay on whatever dish or surface you will be using to hold your piece while it bakes. Follow the directions for a black-and-white transfer and bake.

3. Once your transfer piece is cool, cut out the piano shape with a sharp pair of scissors and then sand around the edges only, using the 320 and 400 grit sandpaper, just to take off the rough edges. Roll out the black clay on the #3 setting of the pasta machine (³⁄₃₂" or 2.4 mm). Put a thin coat of Translucent Liquid Sculpey on the back of the baked white clay that has the transfer image. Then lay the baked white clay piece on top of the black clay you rolled. Cut around the black clay to leave a ⅛" (3 mm) border of black around the white clay shape.

4. Place a very thin line of cyanoacrylate glue along the black clay border. Place the white beads close together on top of the black clay in the line of glue to make an edge around the pin (photo). Press them into the clay. With a small brush, add a tiny bit of Translucent Liquid Sculpey on top of the beads to assure they will stay. Bake and let cool.

5. Sand the back of the piece with all three grits of sandpaper, starting with the 320 grit. Do not buff. Glue on your pin back and the piece is done.

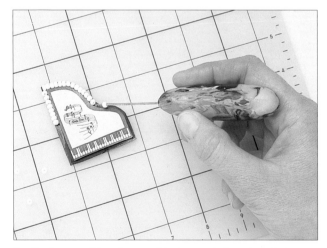

Small white seed beads are added around the edge of the black clay.

ORIENTAL CRACKLE BEADS

Designer
Karen Shiroma, OopsArt!

aren is a polymer clay artist who lives in Hawaii. She has been drawing so long that she can't remember when she started. Her love of polymer clay started about 1993 and has continued to grow ever since. Karen has developed these wonderful crackle-look beads for you to try. Made into a necklace or used as earrings, they are simply gorgeous. The cane slices are placed on a base color of bead, so choose canes that go well with the base colors.

MATERIALS

Polymer clay:

    Gold Premo! Sculpey*

    Pearl Premo! Sculpey*

    A variety of canes

This technique will work only with Premo! Sculpey metallic clays. Gold and pearl appear to work the best, but you might want to experiment with adding the pearl to a small amount of an opaque color, or mixing metallic colors together.

Pasta machine

Sharp blade

Needle tool

Wet/dry sandpaper in 320, 400, and 600 grits

Ice water

Buffing wheel or soft cotton towel

Clay-compatible gloss glaze (optional)

1. Make the Jelly Roll to Prepare the Clay. Roll out a sheet of well-conditioned Premo! gold or pearl on a #4 or #5 setting of the pasta machine (5/64" or 1/16", 2 or 1.6 mm). Make sure the mica in the sheet has shifted so that the entire sheet is bright gold with no dark areas. Fold the outer edges in toward the center of the sheet; then fold the piece in half with the previously folded edges on the inside. Make a jelly roll, starting the roll with the ends that have double folds.

2. Make the Balls. Roll out the jelly roll log into a tapering, carrotlike shape. Cut it into random-size pieces. Pinch each end of these pieces, closing off any of the dark areas. Roll the ends of each piece into the center, and roll each of the pieces into a little ball. The point of doing all of this is to eliminate as much of the dark clay as possible.

3. Making the Beads. Roll out a base bead of gold clay. Place the little balls of gold at random on the base bead, making sure that all of the spaces are covered (Photo 1, left). You can reshape the balls to fit the spaces if you need to. Let the beads rest for approximately 30 minutes before doing the next step. This is to keep the balls from melting into each other and thus losing the crackle pattern.

4. Applying Canes and Baking. Roll the beads with your hands until you have a smooth surface. Slice and apply cane slices here and there. Roll the beads smooth again, or mold into whatever shape you want. Put a hole through each bead with a needle tool. Bake according to the manufacturer's directions. Take the hot beads out of the oven when the baking time is over and drop them into a container of ice water. This helps to clarify the clay and brings out the colors. The crackling effect is not immediately apparent after baking. Sanding and buffing or glazing will bring it out.

5. Finishing. Wet-sand the beads with all three grits of sandpaper, starting with the coarsest. Buff on a buffing wheel or by hand with a soft cotton towel. These beads can also be glazed with a gloss type clay-compatible glaze.

Upper left: Small balls of gold clay were added to a base bead. Center: Thin cane slices are added to the smoothed ball of clay.

BOGUS BEAD NECKLACE

Designer
Dotty McMillan

The earth has given us some wonderful gifts in the form of precious and semiprecious stones. Jewelry makers have, since the beginning of time, used these gifts to make beads. However, stone beads can be extremely heavy, both in price and weight. Polymer clay is much lighter than the real thing, so beads made with it are far more comfortable to wear than the real thing. Clay beads are also lighter in price. So for comfort as well as for your budget, why not make them from polymer clay?

See the Great Impostors section of the book for the specifics of making jade, turquoise, and rose quartz shown in this project, or make your beads look like any of the other great impostors you like.

MATERIALS

Polymer clay:

Translucent, 3 oz (84 g)

Turquoise, 2 oz (56 g)

Small amounts of black, purple, green, alizarin crimson or bordeaux red, and orange

Contrasting color for small spacer beads, 1 oz (28 g)

Square of acrylic plastic 3" × 3" (7.5 × 7.5 cm), or a smooth jar lid from a wide-mouthed jar, such as a peanut butter jar

Needle tool

Sharp blade

Polyester stuffing (the kind used to stuff teddy bears), a few small handfuls

Wet/dry sandpaper in 320, 400, and 600 grits

Buffing wheel or soft cotton towel

Bead roller (optional), available from some clay suppliers

SoftFlex® nylon-covered stainless steel wire or other bead wire, findings, and seed beads (optional) in your choice of colors

1. Turquoise Beads. Follow the directions for making faux turquoise in Great Impostors, using an amount of clay that will make each bead approximately 1" (2.5 cm) in diameter. Make three beads. Put a hole through them with your needle tool. Bake on polyester stuffing. Let cool. Sand with all three grits of wet sandpaper, starting with the coarsest, and buff.

2. Jade Beads

a. Follow the directions in Great Impostors for making the faux jade, using translucent clay and a small amount of green clay, plus a tiny bit of orange clay to desaturate the green color and make it grayer. Divide the clay into four sections, large enough to make four beads that are 1" (2.5 cm) in diameter. Add a very tiny amount of purple and marble it through all four of the green clay pieces. You only want a slight streak of it here and there. Roll each piece into a smooth ball. Grate tiny bits of black clay onto your work surface. Then roll each bead so that a few pieces of the black adhere to it.

b. Using either the acrylic square or the jar lid, roll a bicone bead (oval tapering to a cone at each end) as follows: Hold the lid from the top with your thumb and all four fingers (Photo 1). Press down slightly and begin rolling in one direction. This takes a little practice, but once you get the hang of it, it's easy. If your bicone is slightly off kilter, you can straighten it with your fingers.

1. Hand position for rolling bicone beads.

c. Put a hole through each bead from pointed tip to pointed tip (Photo 2). Bake beads on a bed of polyester stuffing and let cool. Sand with all three grits of wet sandpaper and buff.

3. Rose Quartz. Make rose quartz clay, following the directions for making rose quartz in Great Impostors. Roll four smooth round balls and put a hole through them with your needle tool. Bake on polyester stuffing and let cool. Sand with wet sandpaper and buff. Alternate shape: If you have a bead roller, you can roll these into football shapes instead of making them round. If you slice off the tips of the football shape, you will have a barrel type bead, which you might wish to use.

2. Faux turquoise, jade, and rose quartz beads.

4. Stringing. Starting with one of the turquoise beads, place it in the middle of the wire, and add beads as shown in the photograph. You can string them next to each other or you can place several seed beads or polymer clay spacers in between each bead, as shown. You can lengthen or shorten your necklace by adding or subtracting seed beads. Add the findings to finish.

3. Beads may be strung with polymer clay spacers in between.

Gallery of Artists' Work

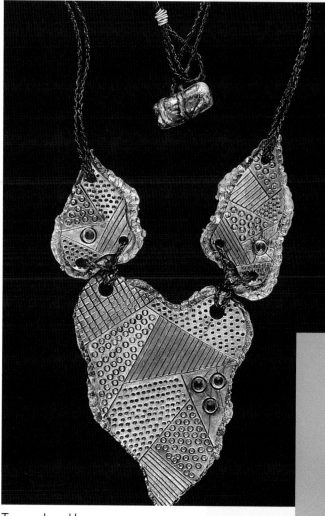

Textured necklace
by Syndee Holt.

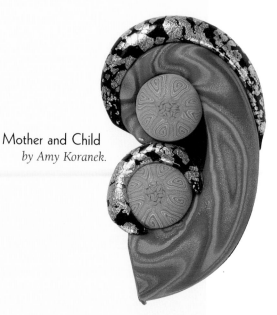

Mother and Child
by Amy Koranek.

Untitled
by Margaret Reid.

Untitled
*by Ilysa
Ginsburg
Bierer.*

Untitled
by Carol Jong.

Tiny vessel made over
medication bottle
by Jody Bishel.

Japanese inro
by Dotty McMillan.

Pens and pencils
by Jami Miller.

Untitled
by Barbara McGuire.

Carved look bead
by Dotty McMillan.

Namibian earrings
by Louise Fischer Cozzi.

Mask
by Carol Zilliacus

Untitled
by Carol Zilliacus.

Untitled
by Barbara McGuire.

Goblet
by Marie Segal.

Pendant
by Marie Segal.

Namibian "Harry" necklace
by Louise Fischer Cozzi.

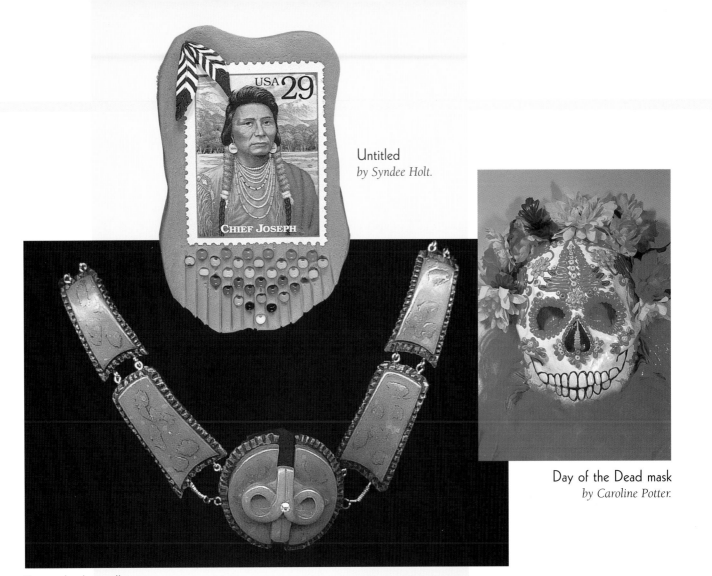

Untitled
by *Syndee Holt.*

Day of the Dead mask
by *Caroline Potter.*

Faux jade dog collar
by *Pauline Hagino.*

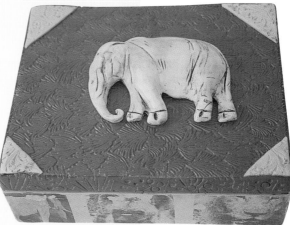

Elephant box
by *Dotty McMillan.*

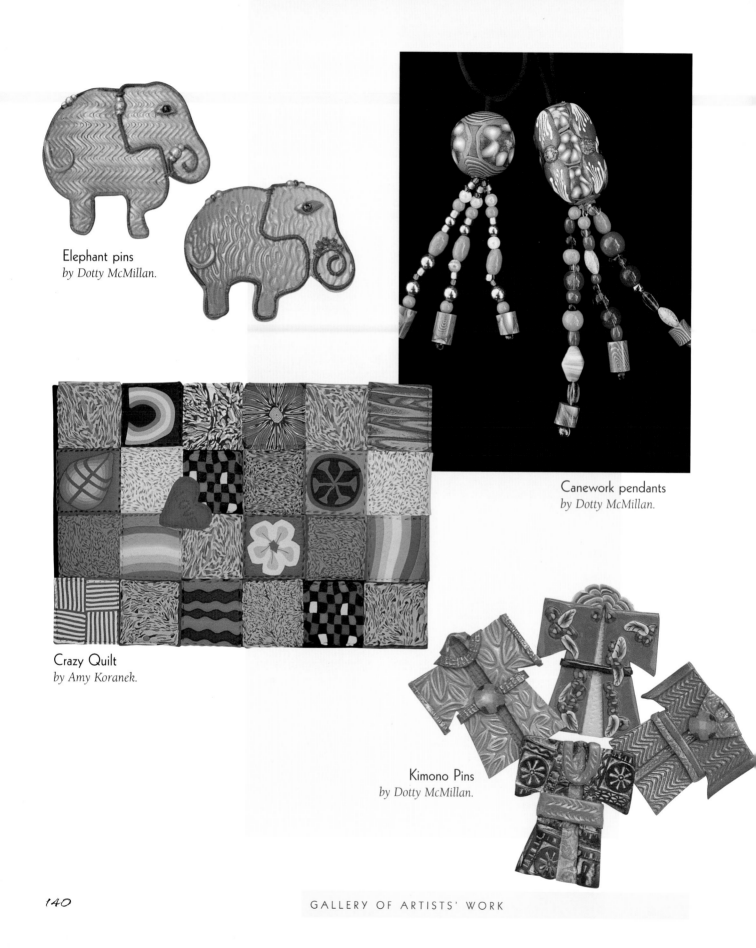

Elephant pins
by Dotty McMillan.

Canework pendants
by Dotty McMillan.

Crazy Quilt
by Amy Koranek.

Kimono Pins
by Dotty McMillan.

Anyone for Shoes?
by Deborah Anderson.

Crafty Lady
by Jeanne Rhea.

Fanciful Figure
by Kathy Davis.

Going Buggy
by Dotty McMillan.

Dragon Box
by Syndee Holt.

Untitled
by Kathy Davis.

Untitled
by Randi Taylor.

Index